TWO SPIRITS

Two Spirits-the Divine Spirit and the Human Spirit

A LESSON BOOK - LEVEL THREE

*Based on and Compiled from
the Writings of*

WATCHMAN NEE
AND
WITNESS LEE

Living Stream Ministry
Anaheim, California

First Edition, June 1990.

ISBN 0-87083-523-8

Published by

Living Stream Ministry
2431 W. La Palma Ave., Anaheim, CA 92801 U.S.A.
P. O. Box 2121, Anaheim, CA 92814 U.S.A.

Printed in the United States of America

04   05   06   07   08   09   /   12   11   10   9   8   7   6   5

TABLE OF CONTENTS

Concerning the Divine Spirit

Concerning the Human Spirit

INTRODUCTION
TO THE LESSON BOOK

Concerning the Lesson Books

This lesson book is one in a series originally designed to teach the truth to junior high and high school students during their summer school of the truth. Because the lesson books were written over a period of several years, the books may vary in style and format.

Concerning This Lesson Book

This is the third lesson book in this series. This book is based upon and compiled from the writings of Brother Witness Lee and he has not reviewed it.

In the previous lesson book concerning the Triune God and the Person and work of Christ, we saw that our God is wonderfully triune so that He can dispense Himself into us. The Bible reveals that God the Father is the planner, God the Son is the accomplisher, and God the Spirit is the applier of all He has planned and accomplished. In this lesson book we shall see in more detail the matter of the Spirit being the applier. It is the all-inclusive, life-giving Spirit who makes the Triune God so real and experiential to us.

We shall also see the vital key to enjoying this all-inclusive Spirit: the human spirit. The human spirit is the strategic point of God's full salvation. The divine dispensing begins with the regeneration of our spirit and continues from our spirit into our soul in the processes of sanctification and transformation. Our spirit is the residence of the Spirit of God! The divine Spirit is wonderful and available, but if we do not know about our human spirit, He is very hard to experience.

In these two spirits—the divine Spirit and the human spirit—we can see God's entire economy; that is, the processed Triune God as the Spirit desires to dispense Himself into the tripartite man to produce the Body of Christ. If we wish to be in this divine economy and enjoy such a dispensing, we must know about these two spirits. This dispensing is also what every man needs, and so we have a responsibility to tell others about it. We pray that you would immerse yourself in these truths and immerse yourself in the Spirit! Then you should go and tell the world of this!

The Structure of the Lessons

The title conveys the subject of the lesson. The verses are for reading or pray-reading. The outline gives you an overview of the lesson. It is good to read the outline first to get an overview of the lesson before you proceed to the text of the lesson. The text is organized according to the outline. The writing contained inside the brackets [ ] are quotes from Brother Lee's publications. The questions are intended to help you better understand and apprehend the lesson. A list of books with the author, publisher, and page number is included for all quoted materials. Finally, a list of books is included for further reference on the subject of each lesson. Lee represents Brother Witness Lee. LSM represents Living Stream Ministry.

The Versions Used in Quotes

When quoting verses, we used the American Standard Version of the Bible for the Old Testament and the Recovery Version of the Bible for the New Testament. We sometimes replaced New Testament quotations found inside the brackets [ ] with the corresponding Recovery Version verse.

The Proper Attitude Needed to Study the Word with the Help of the Lesson Book

This lesson book is not the Bible. It is a lesson book based on the Bible. It can be used as a study aid for the Bible. Do not quote the lesson book as the authoritative source for biblical truths or teachings. You must learn to reference the appropriate source—which book, which chapter, and which verse, etc. You must also learn how all the key verses relate to one another in presenting the vision of the church and the way to build up the church. Take the time to know the Word of God with certainty.

The Way to Study the Word with This Lesson Book

The Word of God embodies the essence of the Spirit. Therefore, when you come to the Word, you must use your spirit. The best way to use your spirit is to pray. You must pray before, during, and after the studying of this lesson book. It is also important that you fellowship as you are studying. It is not adequate to read by yourself without fellowshipping with others. The fellowship of the Body is necessary to help you comprehend the heavenly vision.

Suggestions on the Summer School of the Truth

It is suggested that the summer school of the truth be six weeks in length. Each week should be divided into four days, each day lasting three hours. Twenty-four days, each with three hours, will provide adequate time to pray, to cover all the lessons, and to fellowship. We recommend that all the students practice to write prophecies for each lesson, and also practice prophesying to speak for Christ and speak forth Christ. Each student should endeavor to experience individually and corporately what he has learned.

We have prayed and will continue to pray for you, that you may have an enjoyable time together during your summer school of the truth, that you will progress towards the full knowledge of the truth, and be built up in your locality. Amen!

June, 1990   Paul Hon

Pleasant Hill, California

THE TWO SPIRITS

Scripture Reading

John 3:6; 4:24; Rom. 8:16; Gen. 1:26; Eph. 1:10; 3:9;
1 Tim. 6:16; John 1:14; 20:22; 14:17

Outline

I. God's eternal purpose
   A. A people to express God
   B. Man being made in God's image
II. The way God fulfills His eternal purpose
   A. God's economy (*oikonomia*)
   B. God's dispensing of Himself to produce the Body
III. God as the Spirit reaching man
   A. The way God can enter into the believers
   B. The Spirit being the transmission of God
IV. The Spirit being the entire Triune God
V. The Spirit of reality
VI. The human spirit
   A. For contacting God
   B. Being the key to the Christian life
   C. The greatness of man's spirit

Text

In the New Testament there are three verses that speak of
both the human spirit and the divine Spirit. They are important verses that you should memorize. They are John 3:6,
John 4:24, and Romans 8:16.

[In John 3:6 we read: "That which is born of the Spirit is
spirit." This verse speaks of two distinct "spirits": one is capitalized and the other is not. The first occurrence of the word
refers to the Holy Spirit of God, and the second to the human
spirit of man. That which is born of the Holy Spirit is the
human spirit. Another verse showing these two "spirits" is
John 4:24: "God is Spirit; and those who worship Him must

worship in spirit and reality." Again, the first "Spirit" is capitalized and the second is not. We must worship God, who is the Spirit, in our human spirit. Romans 8:16 further confirms the existence of two spirits: "The Spirit Himself witnesses with our spirit that we are the children of God." The pronoun "our" definitely designates the human spirit and removes any ground to doubt the reality of both the divine Spirit and the human spirit.]

Many who have been Christians for years have never seen the two spirits in these verses. Yet, this is a crucial truth concerning God, His purpose, and our Christian experience.

I. GOD'S ETERNAL PURPOSE

A. A People to Express God

[According to Ephesians 3, in eternity past God planned to work Himself into His chosen people. His eternal purpose is to have a people with Him as life. God will be within them and they will be one with Him. This people will be the Body of Christ to express God Himself in Christ. First they are the church and eventually the New Jerusalem.]

B. Man Being Made in God's Image

[The Bible tells us that in eternity past there was only God. Then He purposed to have a Body for Christ. For this He created the universe and then man, the center of the universe. Man, Genesis 1:26 tells us, was made in a specific way. He was made in God's image and according to His likeness. Why was it that God made man in His own form? It was because God intended that one day He would enter man to make man His container, with Himself as the content. From the very beginning, then, from the time of man's creation, the preparation was made for man to contain God.]

II. THE WAY GOD FULFILLS
HIS ETERNAL PURPOSE

A. God's Economy (*Oikonomia*)

The way in which God fulfills His eternal purpose is His "economy." [The economy of God is to dispense Himself into

His chosen, predestinated, and redeemed people as their life, their life supply, and their everything. We have spent much time to study the Greek word for economy or dispensation used in Ephesians 1:10; 3:9 and 1 Timothy 1:4—*oikonomia.* This Greek word is a compound word made up of *oikos,* meaning house, and *nomos,* meaning law. If you trace the root of this word, it goes back to a word that refers to the parceling out of food, the distributing of food as in parcels. This root word also means to distribute food to the cattle for grazing. It is God's economy to parcel Himself out to us as our life and as our life supply.]

B. God's Dispensing of Himself to Produce the Body

[In God's economy He dispenses Himself into His people as life, as life supply, and as everything to them. He dispenses Himself as their strength, their power, their wisdom, their righteousness, their holiness, their love, their kindness, and even as their attributes and virtues. This is God's economy. Out of this economy many believers are being produced to be the components of the Body of God's Son for a full expression of the Triune God. This is our vision concerning God's economy.]

III. GOD AS THE SPIRIT REACHING MAN

A. The Way God Can Enter into the Believers

In what way could the infinite God be dispensed into man? [The Father by Himself cannot reach us, nor can the Son by Himself enter into us. The Father is unapproachable (1 Tim. 6:16), but the Son came to tabernacle among us (John 1:14). But still He was not able to enter into us because He was blood and flesh. As a man with a physical body He was able to be among His disciples, but not within them. So He told His disciples that He had to die and to be raised up. By His death and resurrection His form was changed from a physical form into a spiritual form. He became the pneumatic Christ who was able to enter into His disciples (John 20:22). This is the reaching of the Triune God. When the Triune God reaches His redeemed people, He is the Spirit.]

B. The Spirit Being the Transmission of God

[God the Father is embodied in God the Son, and God the Son is realized, transmitted, experienced and gained by us in God the Spirit. The Spirit as the third in the Godhead is God being our realization and experience. This means that the application of the Triune God to us comes by the Spirit of God. For this reason, in our experience the Triune God is the Spirit.

Electrical current is an illustration of the Spirit as the application of the Triune God. Apart from the current of electricity, electricity cannot be applied. In its application, electricity needs to become an electrical current. The current, however, is not something different from electricity itself. The current of electricity is simply electricity in motion. In the same principle, the application of the Triune God to us is the Spirit. The Spirit is the current of the Triune God for us to apply; He is the Triune God in motion.]

IV. THE SPIRIT BEING THE ENTIRE TRIUNE GOD

Furthermore, [it is very important to see that the Father and the Son are fully realized in the Spirit as the third of the Godhead. This means that we cannot separate the Holy Spirit from the Son or the Father. The three of the Godhead not only coexist, but They also coinhere. Hence, among the Father, Son, and Spirit there are both coexistence and coinherence. God is triune; He is three-one.] We have covered these matters quite thoroughly in the Triune God lesson book.

[The Holy Spirit is the ultimate and consummate reaching of the Triune God to us. Do not think that when the Holy Spirit reaches you, only He, the third of the Godhead, comes, and that the Father and the Son remain in heaven. Some Christians have such an understanding. Instead of believing that Christ is in us, they claim that Christ sent the Holy Spirit to function as His representative in us. This concept is altogether wrong. The Bible does not speak of the Spirit representing the Son in the believers. On the contrary, according to the Scriptures, when the Holy Spirit comes, the Son comes with Him and in Him. The Father also comes with the

Son and the Spirit. This means that when the Holy Spirit comes to us, the entire Triune God comes. According to the Bible, we may say that the Father is the source, the Son is the course, and the Spirit is the flow. How marvelous that the Holy Spirit is the consummate reaching of the Triune God to you and me!]

V. THE SPIRIT OF REALITY

Because the Spirit is the realization of the Triune God, He is called the Spirit of reality (John 14:17; 15:26; 16:13). [In John 16:13 we see that the Spirit of reality guides us into all the reality: "But when He, the Spirit of reality, comes, He will guide you into all the reality; for He will not speak from Himself, but whatever he hears He will speak; and he will disclose to you what is to come." The Spirit of reality guides the believers into all the reality of the Triune God and of all divine matters. The Spirit of reality guides us into the reality of justification, holiness, love, and all other divine things. He leads us into, brings us into, the reality of these things.]

[If we would apply all that God and Christ are, we need the Spirit. We must praise the Lord that today He is not only the Father and the Son but also the Spirit. He is not only the source and the course but also the application. The Spirit reaches us, entering into us and applying all that we need of the Father and the Son. This is wonderful.]

VI. THE HUMAN SPIRIT

A. For Contacting God

[Man can be likened to a radio. The Spirit of God is like the heavenly radio waves. The spirit in man is like the radio receiver. Many radios do not function because their owners do not use their spirit! People are unable to contact God because the receiver within them is out of order.] If man did not have a spirit, he would be unable to contact God.

B. Being the Key to the Christian Life

[It is in our spirit that we were born again (John 3:6); it is in our spirit that we were made alive (Eph. 2:5; Rom. 8:10); it is in our spirit that God dwells (Eph. 2:22; 2 Tim. 4:22; Rom. 8:16); it is in our spirit that we are joined to the Lord (1 Cor. 6:17); and it is in our spirit that we contact and worship God (John 4:24). Now we must walk and have our whole being according to our spirit—serving in our spirit (Rom. 1:9), praying in spirit (Eph. 6:18), being filled in spirit (Eph. 5:18), seeing God's revelation in spirit (Eph. 1:17; 3:5; Rev. 1:10; 4:2; 17:3; 21:10), having fellowship with the brothers and sisters in spirit (Phil. 2:1); and being built together with others into a dwelling place of God in spirit (Eph. 2:22).]

C. The Greatness of Man's Spirit

[Zechariah 12:1 tells us that there are three crucial things in God's creation: the heavens, the earth, and the spirit of man. It says that Jehovah is the One who "stretches forth the heavens, and lays the foundation of the earth, and forms the spirit of man within him." How great is our spirit! The heavens are for the earth. Without the heavens, the earth could not have anything organic. The earth is for man, and man is for God. For man to be for God, he needs a receiver. This receiver is our human spirit. Praise the Lord that we are here under God's plan and in His plan; that we have been made by Him in His image and after His likeness; that we have a spirit to receive Him; and that He, as the divine Spirit, has entered into our human spirit, making us His sons for His expression! This is His plan.]

SUMMARY

God's eternal purpose is to have a people that would express Him. The way He fulfills this purpose is called His economy. In His economy, God as the Spirit dispenses Himself into man. God is able to dispense Himself into man because He is the Spirit and man has a spirit. The Spirit transmits the entire Triune God, and the human spirit receives this transmission. Our spirit is the means for us to contact the Triune God; therefore the human spirit is a great thing in the universe. By the divine Spirit entering the human spirit, God will accomplish His desire.

Questions

1. Name the three New Testament verses that speak of both the divine Spirit and the human spirit. What do they say?

2. What is God's eternal purpose?

3. How will God fulfill His purpose?

4. What does the Greek word "oikonomia" mean?

5. How can the great God get Himself into man?

6. Is the Spirit merely a third of the Godhead?

7. Why is the Spirit called "the Spirit of reality" in John's writings?

8. What is the significance of the human spirit?

Quoted Portions
from (Lee/LSM) Publications

1. *The Economy of God*, p. 26.

2. *The Completing Ministry of Paul*, p. 9.

3. *The Vision of the Lord's Recovery, Elders' Training, Book 2*, pp. 17-18.

4. *The Divine Dispensing of the Divine Trinity*, p. 26.

5. *Life-study of Romans*, pp. 578-579.

6. *Life-study of Philippians*, pp. 335-337.

7. *The Fulfillment of the Tabernacle and the Offerings in the Writings of John*, p. 413.

8. *Life-study of John*, pp. 445-446.

9. *Life Messages*, p. 613.

10. *Our Human Spirit*, p. 5.

11. *The Basic Revelation in the Holy Scriptures*, p. 18.

Lesson Two

THE ALL-INCLUSIVE SPIRIT

Scripture Reading

Gen. 1:2; Ezek. 11:5; Luke 1:35; John 7:37-39; Acts 16:6-7; Rom. 8:9-11; Phil. 1:9; Rev. 22:17

Outline

I. The progressive revelation of the divine Spirit
   A. The Spirit of God
   B. The Spirit of Jehovah
   C. The Holy Spirit
   D. The Spirit being "not yet"
   E. The Spirit of Jesus
   F. The Spirit of Christ
   G. The Spirit of Jesus Christ
II. The Spirit—the all-inclusive, processed Triune God
III. Saved by the bountiful supply of the Spirit

Text

We have seen that because God is Spirit, He can reach man and enter into him. For God to get into man, however, was not a simple matter. The Triune God went through a great process in order to dispense Himself into us. We can see this from the revelation of the Bible concerning the divine Spirit.

I. THE PROGRESSIVE REVELATION OF THE DIVINE SPIRIT

[The revelation in the Bible concerning God, Christ, and the Spirit is progressive. This revelation begins in Genesis 1 and develops progressively until it reaches its consummation in the book of Revelation.]

A. The Spirit of God

[The first mention of the Spirit in the Scriptures is found

in Genesis 1:2, where we are told that the Spirit of God was
brooding over the waters (Heb.). In relation to God's creation,
the Spirit is specifically called the Spirit of God.]

B. The Spirit of Jehovah

[God's relationship with man, of course, is more intimate
than His relationship with creation.] [After creating man,
God remained intimately involved with him. In His relation-
ship with man God's title is Jehovah. This is why in the Old
Testament the Spirit of God is usually called the Spirit of
Jehovah. The Spirit of Jehovah came upon certain people.
This indicates that the Spirit of Jehovah has to do with God's
reaching of man (Judg. 3:10; Ezek. 11:5). The main titles used
for the Spirit of God in the Old Testament are the Spirit of
God and the Spirit of Jehovah.]

C. The Holy Spirit

The first divine title given to the Spirit in the New Testament is the "Holy Spirit." [At the incarnation the Spirit of
God was called the Holy Spirit (Matt. 1:18, 20; Luke 1:35).
Andrew Murray in his masterpiece, *The Spirit of Christ,*
points out that the divine title, the Holy Spirit, is not used in
the Old Testament. In Psalm 51:11 and in Isaiah 63:10-11 the
"Holy Spirit" should be translated "the Spirit of holiness." It
was when the time came to prepare the way for Christ's
coming and to prepare a human body for Him to initiate the
New Testament dispensation, that the term "Holy Spirit"
came into use (Luke 1:15, 35).]

[Luke 1:35 gives us the first mention of the Holy Spirit. He
is introduced at the time when the Lord Jesus was conceived
by a human mother. This is because something common is to
be made holy. In this same verse the One to be born is called
"that holy thing." The Holy Spirit came into a human being to
conceive something holy. When the Holy Spirit came into us
common human beings, we too could be made holy.]

D. The Spirit Being Not Yet

Now we come to a very puzzling but crucial point in the

gradual revelation of the Spirit. [In John 7:37-38 the Lord Jesus cried, "If anyone thirst, let him come to Me and drink. He who believes in Me, as the Scriptures said, out of his innermost being shall flow rivers of living water." Then in verse 39 John explains that the Lord spoke this "concerning the Spirit, whom those who believed in Him were about to receive; for the Spirit was not yet, because Jesus was not yet glorified." John does not say the Spirit of God, the Spirit of Jehovah, or the Holy Spirit, but "the Spirit." He further says that when Jesus was crying out to the people, "the Spirit was not yet." The King James Version says, "the Spirit was not yet *given*," but the word "given" is inserted; it is not in the Greek text. The Spirit of God was in Genesis 1, and the Spirit of Jehovah came upon the prophets in the Old Testament. Why, then, in John 7 was the Spirit "not yet"?]

[In chapter seven of John, the Lord Jesus was still in the flesh; He was not yet in glory, that is, not yet in resurrection. Because He was not yet resurrected, the Spirit was not yet. Of course, the Spirit of God existed from the very beginning (Gen. 1:1-2), but the Spirit as the Spirit of Jesus (Acts 16:7), the Spirit of Christ (Rom. 8:9), and the Spirit of Jesus Christ (Phil. 1:19), was "not yet" until the Lord was glorified in resurrection. After His resurrection, the Spirit of God became the Spirit of the incarnated, crucified, and resurrected Jesus Christ. This involves the matter of process.

In Genesis 1:2 we have the Spirit of God. The only element in the Spirit of God is the divine essence. But after the incarnation, crucifixion, and resurrection of the Lord Jesus, the Spirit became the Spirit of Jesus, the Spirit of Christ, and the Spirit of Jesus Christ. When the Spirit of God was just the Spirit of God, the only element in the Spirit was the divine essence. But when the Spirit of God became the Spirit of Jesus, the essence of humanity was added.]

E. The Spirit of Jesus

[According to Acts 16:6, Paul and his co-workers were "forbidden of the Holy Spirit to preach the Word in Asia." But verse 7 says that the Spirit of Jesus did not allow them to go

into Bithynia. In these two verses first we have the Holy
Spirit, then the Spirit of Jesus. If we study the context of
verse 7, we shall see that Paul was suffering. For this reason,
the Spirit of Jesus was with him. The Spirit of Jesus has
the elements of humanity, human living, and crucifixion.
Because Paul in Acts 16 was experiencing human suffering
and was experiencing the death of Christ, the Spirit of God,
the Spirit of the Lord, and the Holy Spirit at that juncture
were the Spirit of Jesus, the Spirit of the incarnated One who
lived on earth as a man and died on the cross.]

F. The Spirit of Christ

[Romans 8:9 says, "But you are not in the flesh, but in the
spirit, if indeed the Spirit of God dwells in you. But if anyone
has not the Spirit of Christ, he is not of Him." Verses 9, 10,
and 11 of Romans 8 are concerned with the resurrection of
Christ. The Spirit of Christ in verse 9 has the element of
resurrection. This Spirit is the Spirit of God mentioned in the
same verse and also the Spirit of life mentioned in verse 2.

In the Spirit we have Christ's incarnation, humanity,
human living, death, and resurrection. This is revealed by the
different titles of the Spirit. If the Spirit did not contain the
elements of incarnation, human living, and crucifixion, why
would He be called the Spirit of Jesus? Likewise, if the Spirit
did not contain the element of resurrection, why would He be
called the Spirit of Christ? Furthermore, if the Spirit did not
contain the divine life, why would He be called the Spirit of
life? The titles of the Spirit denote certain facts. Therefore,
based on the titles of the Spirit used in the New Testament,
we can say that in the Spirit of Jesus we have incarnation,
humanity, human living, suffering, and crucifixion, and in the
Spirit of Christ we have resurrection, the power of resurrection, and the divine life.]

G. The Spirit of Jesus Christ

[In Philippians 1:19 Paul speaks of the Spirit of Jesus
Christ: "For I know that for me this shall turn out to salvation
through your petition and the bountiful supply of the Spirit of

Jesus Christ." When Paul wrote this word, he was in prison. But even though he was a prisoner, he could rejoice because he had the bountiful supply of the Spirit of Jesus Christ. He enjoyed the Spirit of Jesus, the suffering One, and the Spirit of Christ, the resurrected One. This Spirit supplied and supported Paul in his suffering and enabled him to rejoice. Therefore, Paul could say in Philippians 1:20 and 21, "According to my earnest expectation and hope that in nothing I shall be put to shame, but with all boldness, as always, even now Christ shall be magnified in my body, whether through life or through death; for to me to live is Christ, and to die is gain."]

II. THE SPIRIT—
THE ALL-INCLUSIVE, PROCESSED TRIUNE GOD

When all the aspects and elements of the Spirit are put together we have a totality, a final product known in the New Testament as "the Spirit" (Rom. 8:16, 23, 26, 27; Gal. 3:14; 5:16-18, 22, 25; 1 Pet. 1:2; Rev. 2:7; 14:13; 22:17). This wonderful Spirit eventually becomes so simple in title! He is simple in title but full of divine elements for our enjoyment. This Spirit is the Spirit of God, the Spirit of Jehovah, the Holy Spirit, the Spirit of Jesus, the Spirit of Christ, and the Spirit of Jesus Christ. He is now the all-inclusive, compound, life-giving, indwelling Spirit who is the processed Triune God.

[We have seen that at the time of John 7:39, the Spirit was "not yet." That was before the Lord Jesus was crucified and glorified in resurrection. But now we who believe in Christ may fulfill our destiny of enjoying the Spirit, and this Spirit will become rivers of living water flowing out of our innermost being. According to John 7:38 and 39, the Spirit, the all-inclusive Spirit, will become rivers of living water flowing out of us. This means that in our experience the one Spirit becomes many rivers of living water. This is the enjoyment of the Spirit.]

III. SAVED BY THE BOUNTIFUL SUPPLY
OF THE SPIRIT

[In Philippians 1 Paul was saved from a particular situation through the bountiful supply of the Spirit. In chapter two he goes on to point out how the believers may experience a constant salvation in the ordinary things of daily life. For example, 2:14 says, "Do all things without murmurings and reasonings." Murmurings and reasonings are things we experience daily. We may not experience hate or anger every day, but we certainly reason and murmur every day.]

You may often be unhappy with your situation at home or at school. You feel you are too restricted or overworked; you need more freedom or a change of pace. This kind of thinking, however, does not change things or make you happier. What you really need is the bountiful supply of the all-inclusive Spirit! Paul was in prison expecting to die, yet he was rejoicing (Phil. 4:4). He said, "I have learned, in whatever circumstances I am, to be content" (Phil. 4:11). The next time that you feel your situation is a "prison," you need to declare, "Praise the Lord! Thank You for my wonderful situation! Dear Lord, You are all that I need!" This is not a theory; it is practical and experiential. This will save you from so many negative things and will surely cause you to express Christ to those around you.

SUMMARY

The revelation in the Bible concerning the Spirit is progressive. In the Old Testament, the Spirit is merely the Spirit of God and the Spirit of Jehovah. It is not until the time of the Lord's incarnation in the New Testament that the title "Holy Spirit" is used. The "Spirit of God" existed from the very beginning, but "the Spirit" was "not yet" until the Lord passed through the process of incarnation, human living, death and resurrection. The Spirit today is the all-inclusive Spirit containing all the divine elements for our enjoyment!

Questions

1. What are the main titles used for the Spirit of God in the Old Testament? To what are they related?

2. When is the term "Holy Spirit" first used?

3. Why in John 7 was the Spirit "not yet?"

4. What are the elements of the Spirit of Jesus? The Spirit of Christ?

5. What is the consummate title of the divine Spirit? What is included in this simple title?

Quoted Portions
from (Lee/LSM) Publications

1. *Life-study of Philippians*, p. 41.

2. *The Basic Revelation in the Holy Scriptures*, pp. 33-34.

3. *The Completing Ministry of Paul*, p. 50.

4. *The Basic Revelation in the Holy Scriptures*, p. 34.

5. *The Fulfillment of the Tabernacle and the Offerings in the Writings of John*, p. 380.

6. *Life-study of Exodus*, pp. 1727-1728, 1730.

7. *Life-study of Philippians*, pp. 424-425.

Lesson Three

THE COMPOUND SPIRIT

Scripture Reading

Exo. 30: 22-25; Psa. 45:7; Isa. 61:1; Col. 3:5;
Gal. 5:24; Rom. 8:13; John 7:39

Outline

I. The compound ointment in Exodus 30
II. The significance of the ingredients
   A. Olive oil
   B. Myrrh
   C. Cinnamon
   D. Calamus
   E. Cassia
III. The significance of the numbers and measurements
   A. One hin of oil with four spices
   B. Three units of five hundred
   C. Five elements
IV. The compounded Spirit

Text

I. THE COMPOUND OINTMENT IN EXODUS 30

In the last lesson we saw that the divine Spirit was only the Spirit of God and the Spirit of Jehovah in the Old Testament. The all-inclusive Spirit was "not yet" because the Triune God had not yet passed through the steps of His process. Yet Exodus 30:22-25 shows a marvelous picture that signifies the all-inclusive Spirit. "Moreover Jehovah spoke unto Moses saying, Take thou also unto thee the chief spices: of flowing myrrh five hundred shekels, and of sweet cinnamon half so much, even two hundred and fifty, and of sweet calamus two hundred fifty, and of cassia five hundred...and of olive oil a hin; and thou shalt make a holy anointing oil, a perfume compounded...." (Hin and shekel are ancient units of measure.)

This holy anointing oil was applied to the tabernacle, its contents, and the serving priests. It is a type (symbol) of the "compound Spirit." A compound is something that is the result of the union or mingling of different elements or ingredients. Every ingredient of this compound ointment and its unit of measure shows us something very significant about the Spirit.

II. THE SIGNIFICANCE OF THE INGREDIENTS

A. Olive Oil

[In the Bible olive oil signifies the Spirit of God (Psa. 45:7; Isa. 61:1). Olive oil is produced by the pressing of olives. The olive oil signifies the Spirit of God, through the pressure of Christ's death, flowing out.

The olive oil is the base of the ointment; it is the basic element compounded with the spices. The four spices are compounded into the olive oil to make the ointment. This indicates that the Spirit of God, signified by the olive oil, is no longer merely oil, but now it is oil compounded with certain ingredients.]

B. Myrrh

[Flowing myrrh, smelling sweet but tasting bitter, signifies the precious death of Christ. In the Bible myrrh is used mostly for burial. Hence, myrrh is related to death. According to John 19, when Nicodemus and others were preparing to bury the body of the Lord Jesus, they used myrrh.

Myrrh comes from an aromatic tree. This tree drops its juice either as a result of being cut or through some kind of natural opening or incision. In ancient times, this juice was used to reduce the suffering of death. When the Lord Jesus was being crucified, He was offered wine mixed with myrrh to reduce His pain. However, He refused to take it. No doubt, the myrrh in Exodus 30 is a symbol of the Lord's death.]

C. Cinnamon

Fragrant cinnamon signifies the sweetness and effectiveness of Christ's death. [The effectiveness of Christ's death is
in the Spirit. This Spirit is like an all-inclusive dose of medi-
cine. Some medicines are all-inclusive, containing some
elements that nourish us and other elements that kill germs.
The all-inclusive Spirit is an all-inclusive dose. If we take in
this all-inclusive Spirit, it will heal us, no matter what our
illness is. Within this Spirit is the nourishing element and the
killing element. The killing power of the death of Christ today
is in the all-inclusive Spirit.]

In Colossians 3:5 [Paul says, "Put to death therefore your
members which are on the earth: fornication, uncleanness,
passion, evil desire, and unbridled greedy lust, which is idola-
try." In our sinful members is the law of sin, which makes us
captives of sin and causes our corrupted body to become the
body of death (Rom. 7:23-24). Hence, our members, which are
sinful, are identified with sinful things, such as fornication,
uncleanness, passion, evil desire, and unbridled greedy lust.]

Galatians 5:24 says, "They who are of Christ Jesus have
crucified the flesh with the passions and the lusts." Christ
has accomplished an all-inclusive crucifixion, and we may
now apply it to our lustful flesh. Note, however, that this is
absolutely different from asceticism.

[This corresponds to Romans 8:13: "For if you live according to flesh, you are about to die; but if by the Spirit you put
to death the practices of the body, you will live." By ourselves
we are not able to put to death the practices of the body. Likewise, we are not able to crucify ourselves.] [Our attempts to
put to death the practices of the body are nothing more than
asceticism. Although we are not to practice asceticism, we are
to put to death the negative things in us by the power of the
Holy Spirit. In order to do this, we need to open to the Spirit
and allow the Spirit to flow within us. Through the Spirit's
flowing, we shall experience the effectiveness of Christ's
death. This is not asceticism; it is the operation of the Spirit
within us.]

[We can experience this killing work in our daily lives.

Suppose a brother does not care for the indwelling Spirit, but instead, rejecting the Spirit, quarrels with his wife and says some very unkind things to her. However, suppose this same brother prays himself into the Spirit, lives in the Spirit, and walks in the Spirit. This will make it extremely difficult for him to argue with his wife. As soon as he opens his mouth to quarrel with her, he will experience the element of Christ's death operating within him. Then he finds it impossible to argue with her. Many married brothers have had this kind of experience.] You may not be married, but you should apply this to your own situation with your family and friends.

D. Calamus

[The calamus in Exodus 30 is a reed. The Hebrew root of the word myrrh means flowing, and the root for calamus means standing up. Calamus grows in a marsh or muddy place. But even though it grows in a marsh, it is able to shoot up into the air. According to the sequence of the spices, this calamus signifies the rising up of the Lord Jesus from the place of death. The Lord was put into a marsh, into a death situation, but in resurrection He rose up and stood up. Calamus, therefore, signifies the precious resurrection of Christ.]

E. Cassia

[The fourth spice, cassia, signifies the power of Christ's resurrection. Cassia and cinnamon belong to the same family. Cinnamon is from the inner part of the bark, and cassia, from the outer part of the bark. Both cinnamon and cassia are sweet and fragrant. Furthermore, the plants from which they are derived often live and grow in places where other plants cannot grow.

In ancient times cassia was used as a repellent to drive away insects and snakes. Cassia thus signifies the power, the effectiveness, of Christ's resurrection. Christ's resurrection can withstand any kind of environment, and His resurrection certainly is a repellent. It repels all evil "insects" and especially the old serpent, the Devil.]

[Day by day we must put on the life-giving Spirit as the repellent to Satan. When you call on the name of the Lord Jesus, you not only drink of Him; you also put on the life-giving Spirit as a repellent. If the first thing in the morning you do not put on this repellent, the snake will attack you, and you may lose your temper during the day. But if you call on the Lord's name a few times, you will not only drink of the living water, but also apply the repellent. Whenever you do this, the snake will be frightened.]

III. THE SIGNIFICANCE OF THE NUMBERS AND MEASUREMENTS

A. One Hin of Oil with Four Spices

[In typology numbers are significant. Here in Exodus 30 we have one plus four. In typology the number one signifies the unique God. God, signified by the complete unit of a hin of olive oil, is unique and complete. The number four signifies the creatures. In both Ezekiel 1 and Revelation 4 we read of the four living creatures. Hence, in the Bible the number four always signifies the creatures. Therefore, in this compound ointment we have God signified by the number one and God's creatures signified by the number four. This indicates that the compound ointment is a matter of God plus His creature, man. This reveals that the ointment is compounded with both God and man. God, the basic element, is signified by the olive oil, and man is represented by the four spices.]

B. Three Units of Five Hundred

[In the compound Spirit we also have the Triune God: the Father, the Son, and the Spirit. Perhaps you are wondering how it is possible to see the Triune God typified by the compounded ointment. In this ointment the Triune God is typified by the three units of the measure of the four spices (Exo. 30:23-24). In the compounded ointment there were five hundred shekels of myrrh, two hundred fifty shekels each of cinnamon and calamus, and five hundred shekels of cassia. Although there were four spices, there was a total of three units of five hundred shekels in measure. But how can we apply this to the Triune God? The first unit is five hundred shekels of myrrh. However, the second unit of five hundred shekels is split in half: two hundred fifty shekels of cinnamon and two hundred fifty shekels of calamus. The third unit is five hundred shekels of cassia. Notice that it is the second unit, the middle one, that is split into two parts. Surely this points to the Second of the Triune God, the Son, and to His crucifixion.]

C. Five Elements

Lastly we see the significance of the number five. [The ointment is composed of five basic elements: olive oil, myrrh, cinnamon, calamus, and cassia. The quantity of the spices compounded with the olive oil is one hundred times five. In the Bible the number five, composed of four plus one, is the number of responsibility. Both the ten commandments and the ten virgins are divided into two groups of five (Exo. 34:28-29; Matt. 25:1-2). Look at your hand: You have four fingers and one thumb for the bearing of responsibility. If you had four fingers but no thumb, it would be very difficult to pick up things. Are you the number four or the number five? If God has been added to you, you are number five. I know that I am number five, because God has been added to me. The significance of the number five is that the all-inclusive life-giving Spirit is for the bearing of responsibility. The more you enjoy the all-inclusive Spirit of Christ, the more ability you will have to bear responsibility.]

IV. THE COMPOUNDED SPIRIT

Praise the Lord! The Bible is truly a wonderful book. Those who say that the Bible is not the Word of God have surely never seen the wonderful picture of the compound ointment. By this picture we can more clearly understand why in John 7:39 the Spirit was not yet. Before the Lord's incarnation, human living, crucifixion and resurrection, the Spirit of God was not a compound; He had merely divinity, nothing else. But now, the Spirit is no longer merely the Spirit of God.

[Today the Spirit of God is the Spirit of Jesus, the Spirit of Christ, and the Spirit of Jesus Christ. In this all-inclusive Spirit we enjoy God, the uplifted humanity of Jesus, the sweetness of the death of Christ, the effectiveness of the death of Christ, the resurrection of Christ, and the power of the resurrection of Christ. All these elements are included in this one compound ointment. Remember that the Spirit of Christ is no longer simply the olive oil; it is the compound ointment. This is the processed Spirit. Certainly compounding is a process. Whenever something is compounded, it passes through a process. Hallelujah, today we do not have a Spirit simply composed of divinity alone, but the all-inclusive Spirit compounded with divinity, the humanity of Jesus, the death of Christ, and His resurrection. By our experience we can testify that God, the humanity of Jesus, the effective death of Christ, and the powerful resurrection of Christ are all in the all-inclusive Spirit. This is the Spirit of God compounded with Christ's humanity, death, and resurrection.]

We have covered many points in this lesson. You should take some time to memorize the different ingredients, their measures, and what they symbolize. Making a chart or diagram might help you. This will help you to experience the wonderful compound Spirit in your daily life. Few Christians have realized the matter of the compound Spirit. Thank the Lord that He has opened this great truth to us in these days!

SUMMARY

The compound ointment in Exodus 30 is a type of the "compound Spirit." The olive oil represents the Spirit of God. The four spices symbolize four elements that have been added to the Spirit: myrrh (Christ's death), cinnamon (effectiveness of Christ's death), calamus (Christ's resurrection), and cassia (the power of Christ's resurrection). In the numbers and measurements of the ingredients we also see: 1) the mingling of God and man; 2) the Triune God; and 3) the ability to bear responsibility. All these items are now included in the processed, compound Spirit.

Questions

1. Where do we find the type of the compound Spirit in the Old Testament?

2. Name the ingredients of the compound ointment. What do they signify?

3. How do these ingredients apply to our experience? (Use calamus as an example.)

4. How can we see the mingling of divinity and humanity from the numbers and measurements of the ingredients? How can we see the Triune God? The ability to bear responsibility?

5. What do we mean when we say the Spirit of God was "processed" or "compounded"?

Quoted Portions
from (Lee/LSM) Publications

1. *Life-study of Exodus,* pp. 1689, 1687.

2. *The Spirit and the Body,* p. 32.

3. *Life-study of Colossians,* p. 229.

4. *Life-study of Exodus,* p. 1750.

5. *Life-study of Colossians,* p. 230.

6. *Life-study of Exodus,* pp. 1751, 1688-1689.

7. *The Spirit and the Body,* pp. 33, 28-29.

8. *Life-study of Exodus,* p. 1744.

9. *The Spirit and the Body,* p. 35.

Lesson Four

THE LIFE-GIVING, INDWELLING SPIRIT

Scripture Reading

John 1:1, 14; 1 Cor. 15:45b; 2 Cor. 3:17; John 20:22

Outline

I. The processed God
   A. Becoming a life-giving Spirit
   B. A definite process
II. Christ and the Spirit being one
III. Christ as the indwelling Spirit
IV. Christ never leaving the believers

Text

First Corinthians 15:45b is one of the most crucial verses in the Bible. It says, "The last Adam became a life-giving Spirit." The "last Adam" refers to Christ. The word "became" implies that a process has taken place for Him to be the life-giving Spirit. Today, if you ask people who God is, some will say that He is the Creator. Others may say that He is also our Redeemer and Savior. Not many will say that God is the Spirit.

As the Spirit, God is not simple, for He is the all-inclusive life-giving Spirit. This Spirit includes divinity, humanity, human living, crucifixion, and resurrection. This Spirit is the all-inclusive compound Spirit we saw in the previous lessons.

I. THE PROCESSED GOD

A. Becoming a Life-Giving Spirit

[In eternity past God existed alone. Then, in time, He created all things. At a certain point in history, this creating God, the Creator of all, became a man. This crucial step is called incarnation. By means of incarnation, God put on man with all of creation, for man is the head of creation. The Lord

Jesus, God incarnate, lived on earth for thirty-three and a half years. When He was crucified, all creation was crucified with Him. This means that not only did Christ go to the cross, but the very man God had put on Himself with the entire creation went to the cross with Him. Therefore, Christ's death on the cross was an all-inclusive crucifixion. After His crucifixion, Christ was buried in a tomb. The man and the creation which were crucified with Christ were also buried in that tomb. After three days, Christ arose from the dead in His resurrection. Through resurrection and in resurrection He became the life-giving Spirit. Furthermore, in His ascension to the third heaven, He was crowned and became the Head and the Lord over all. Then He descended upon His Body as the all-inclusive Spirit.

Because God, after completing the work of creation, passed through incarnation, human living, crucifixion, resurrection, ascension, and descension, we may speak of Him as the processed God. The diagram portrays the process through which He has passed.]

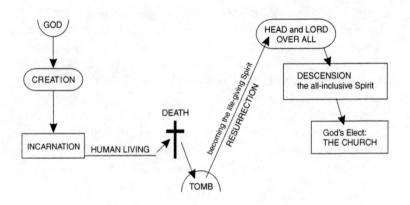

[The Process of the Divine Economy]

B. A Definite Process

[Some find fault with the word "processed" and argue that it is impossible for God to be processed because He is eternal and unchanging. Although God is eternal and unchanging, He has nevertheless passed through a process. Was not incarnation a process? From eternity past until the incarnation of Christ, God did not have a body of flesh. But when He was born in a manger, He was the mighty God incarnated as a baby. According to Isaiah 9:6, the child born to us is called the mighty God....this child, God incarnate, lived in a carpenter's home for years. Imagine that the Creator of the universe lived in the home of a carpenter in Nazareth! Was that not a process? Likewise, were not the crucifixion and resurrection a process? God certainly was processed through Christ's incarnation, human living, crucifixion, and resurrection. Our God today is not a "raw" God, but a processed God. Today He is the all-inclusive life-giving Spirit.]

II. CHRIST AND THE SPIRIT BEING ONE

[First Corinthians 15:45b says that the last Adam became a life-giving Spirit. Second Corinthians 3:17 tells us that now the Lord is the Spirit. The last Adam in 1 Corinthians 15:45b and the Lord in 2 Corinthians 3:17 both refer to Christ. This indicates clearly that today Christ and the Spirit are one.]

[The One who was crucified on the cross was Christ, but the One who entered into the believers was the Spirit. In crucifixion for the believers' redemption He was Christ, but in the indwelling to be the believers' life He is the Spirit. This is the all-inclusive life-giving Spirit, who is the all-inclusive and ultimate blessing of the gospel.] [Because many are not clear concerning this, they talk about a so-called second blessing, or about receiving the Spirit apart from regeneration. When some Christians learn that another has believed in Christ, they proceed to ask him if he has received the Holy Spirit. However, to be a genuine Christian is to believe in Christ and to receive the Spirit. To be a real Christian is to believe in Christ, and to believe in Christ is to receive the Spirit. Nevertheless, those who regard Christ as separate and distinct from the Spirit may consider that it is possible to believe in Christ without receiving the Spirit. This is a serious misunderstanding!]

III. CHRIST AS THE INDWELLING SPIRIT

[When we believed in the Lord Jesus and received Him as our Redeemer, it was the life-giving Spirit who came into us. Many believers do not realize that they received the Lord Jesus not only as the Redeemer and the Savior, but also as the life-giving Spirit. When we believed in the Lord Jesus, we knew that we were sinful. Therefore, we prayed, repented, confessed, and received Him as our Redeemer. However, we were not told that He would come into us to be our life. At least I was not told this when I believed in Him. However, I later found out that after believing in Him, there was something inside me that made me happy and joyful. Sometimes I even felt like leaping. Have you not had this experience? This is the experience of Christ as the life-giving Spirit. Although we received Him as our Redeemer, He came into us not only as our Redeemer, but also as the life-giving Spirit. Today He is in us mainly as the life-giving Spirit.

If you ask believers where their Redeemer, the Lord Jesus, is, many lift up their eyes, point to heaven, and say, "He is in heaven." Rarely do you find a Christian who, when asked where the Lord Jesus is, will say with rejoicing, "Christ is in me!" If you ask me where my Jesus is, I will say, "Jesus my Redeemer is, on the one hand, in the heavens as my Lord and, on the other hand, in me as the life-giving Spirit." For this reason sometimes I am rejoicing, bubbling, and even beside myself with joy. Rejoice, Jesus Christ is the life-giving Spirit within us! Before coming into the churches, you probably never heard that the Redeemer became a life-giving Spirit. But there is a verse in the Bible telling us that the last Adam became the life-giving Spirit. It seems that those in Christianity do not have the second part of 1 Corinthians 15:45. After completing the work of redemption, Christ became the life-giving Spirit.]

IV. CHRIST NEVER LEAVING THE BELIEVERS

John 20 is the first account of the Lord coming to the believers as the life-giving Spirit. The disciples were gathered together in an upper room with all the doors shut for fear of the Jews. Three days earlier they had seen the Lord Jesus crucified.

[Suddenly Jesus was standing among them and saying, "Peace be to you"! His words were few, but He breathed into them and said, "Receive the Holy Spirit" (John 20:22). His words could also be translated, "Receive the holy breath." A few more words, and He was gone. He came in without anyone's opening the door; He left without saying good-bye. It was not that He went away. Rather, He entered into them as the holy breath. From then on, wherever the disciples were, Jesus was also there. He was within them! Here is Christ in resurrection becoming the indwelling Spirit.]

[We can all be assured that this Christ is within us. Wherever we go, He is within. When we are happy with Him, attending the meetings, praying, and pray-reading, we may not have a strong sense that He is within. But if we go against Him, He will appear to us in a strong way. If we go to a movie or to a gambling casino, He will speak to us from within, "What are you doing here?" Our Lord is real, living, present, and within. We do not have a religion. What need have we for a religion? We have the living Christ! He is what we need and what we have.

He is real, living, and powerful, yet kind, loving, and patient. We must not think that if we offend Him, He will leave. The more we offend Him, the more He will convince us that He will never leave!]

The Lord who we should enjoy each day is no longer just in the heavens. He has gone through a great process to become the life-giving Spirit. As such a Spirit, He can come to dwell within our spirit and give life to us. The life He gives is the life of the Triune God Himself. What a Spirit we have! He is the all-inclusive, compound, life-giving, indwelling Spirit who is the processed Triune God!

SUMMARY

The last Adam becoming a life-giving Spirit indicates that God has gone through a process. God has passed through incarnation, human living, crucifixion, and resurrection to become the life-giving Spirit. Christ comes as this Spirit to enter into the believers. This indwelling Christ is within the believers for their experience and will never leave.

Questions

1. How does 1 Corinthians 15:45b show us that God has gone through a process?

2. Diagram the process of the divine economy.

3. Give two verses that show that Christ and the Spirit are one.

4. Where is the Lord Jesus today?

5. Describe how the disciples first received Christ as the life-giving Spirit.

6. After Christ comes to indwell us, will He ever leave?

Quoted Portions
from (Lee/LSM) Publications

1. *Life-study of Colossians,* pp. 219-220, 228.

2. *Life-study of Galatians,* pp. 290-291, 114-117.

3. *The Spirit and the Body,* pp. 21-22.

4. *The Mending Ministry of John,* pp. 15-16.

Lesson Five

THE SEVENFOLD INTENSIFIED SPIRIT

Scripture Reading

Rev. 1:4-5; Zech. 4:2; Rev. 4:5; Exo. 25:37; Rev. 5:6;
Zech. 3:9; Matt. 16:18; 21:42; 1 Pet. 2:4-5

Outline

Text

I. THE SEVEN SPIRITS OF GOD

In this lesson we shall consider the matter of the seven
Spirits of God. The Spirit is mysterious and wonderful
enough without such a term as the "seven Spirits of God."
Nevertheless, the book of Revelation reveals something
further about the Spirit today. Let's read Revelation 1:4-5:
"John to the seven churches which are in Asia: Grace to you
and peace from Him who is, and who was, and who is coming,
and from the seven Spirits who are before His throne, and
from Jesus Christ, the faithful Witness, the Firstborn of the
dead, and the Ruler of the kings of the earth. To Him who
loves us and has loosed us from our sins by His blood."

A. Not Seven Different Spirits

[In the book of Revelation, the age is the age of the Spirit, and in this age the Spirit has been intensified.

Because the Spirit in 1:4 is the intensified Spirit of God, He is called the seven Spirits. The seven Spirits are undoubtedly the Spirit of God because they are ranked among the Triune God in verses 4 and 5. We cannot understand the Bible according to our natural, limited mentality. According to our concept, the words "seven Spirits" denote seven individual spirits. But this is not the meaning. The number seven here does not refer to seven different spirits but to one sevenfold Spirit.]

B. Intensified for God's Move

[Seven is the number of completion in God's dispensational move, while twelve is the number of completion in God's eternal administration. For example, God created the earth in six days plus one Sabbath day. Furthermore, there are seven dispensations in the Bible. For God's move today, the church has the number seven. In the book of Revelation the seven seals, the seven trumpets, and the seven bowls are all for God's dispensational move. Thus, the sevenfold Spirit is the intensified Spirit in God's move today. He is the seven Spirits of God for God's move.

As seven is the number for completion in God's operation, so the seven Spirits are for God's move on the earth. In substance and existence, God's Spirit is one; in the intensified function and work of God's operation, God's Spirit is sevenfold. It is like the lampstand in Zechariah 4:2. In existence it is one lampstand, but in function it is seven lamps. At the time the book of Revelation was written, the church had become degraded and the age had become dark. Therefore, the sevenfold intensified Spirit of God was needed for God's move and work on the earth. We all are familiar with three-way bulbs, light bulbs that can be switched to three successive degrees of illumination. When we do not need very much light, we switch the bulb to the first degree, but when we need more illumination, we switch it to the second or third degree. In like manner, the seven lamps on the lampstand were the sevenfold, intensified light. In the four Gospels, the Spirit of God was one-fold because at that time there was not the need for so much light. However, after the church had been degraded and the age had become exceedingly dark, there was the need for the Holy Spirit to be intensified sevenfold. In this way the one Spirit of God has become the sevenfold Spirit. In existence, the Holy Spirit, like the lampstand in Zechariah, is one, but in function the Holy Spirit is seven.]

II. THE SEVEN LAMPS OF FIRE BURNING BEFORE THE THRONE

Revelation 4:5 [also tells us that "seven lamps of fire are burning before the throne, which are the seven Spirits of God." This indicates that God will touch the earth by the seven lamps, by His seven Spirits which are burning, shining, observing, searching, and judging. The seven lamps here refer to the seven lamps of the lampstand in Exodus 25:37 and the seven lamps of the lampstand in Zechariah 4:2. The seven lamps of fire which are the seven Spirits of God signify the enlightening and searching of the sevenfold intensified Spirit of God. In Exodus 25 and Zechariah 4, the seven lamps, signifying the enlightening of the Spirit of God in God's move, are for God's building, either for the tabernacle or the building of the temple. Here the seven lamps are for God's judgment, which will issue also in God's building—the building of the New Jerusalem. While God executes His judgment, His sevenfold intensified Spirit will carry out God's eternal building by searching, enlightening, judging, and infusing. This is fully developed in the following chapters. The issue is the consummation of the holy city, New Jerusalem.]

III. THE SEVEN EYES OF THE LAMB

Furthermore, in Revelation 5:6, John saw "a Lamb standing as having been slain, having seven horns and seven eyes, which are the seven Spirits of God, sent forth into all the earth."

A. For Moving and Transfusing

[Our eyes are for our moving. If we are blind, it is very

difficult to move. In God's move today, Christ as the Lamb of God has seven eyes. The seven eyes of the Lamb are also for watching, observing, and transfusing. When I look at someone, something of me is transfused into him. We often talk about loving one another; but how can you realize that someone loves you? Love is transfused through the eyes. If you look at me in a loving way, your eyes will transfuse your love into me. When Christ looks at us with His seven eyes, we may be terrified at first. Eventually, however, these seven eyes will transfuse Christ's element into us.]

B. Not Separate from Christ

[The Holy Spirit today is the seven eyes of Christ. Many Christians argue that the Holy Spirit of God is separate from Christ, but the Bible says that the Holy Spirit is the eyes of Christ. Do you think of your eyes as being separate from you? It is ridiculous to say this. When I look at your eyes, I look at you, and when you look at me with your eyes, you look me. The eyes of a person express that person. To say that the Holy Spirit is separate from Christ does not correspond with the pure revelation of the Holy Word.]

[Day by day, we sense that Someone is looking at us. This Someone is the Spirit, who is Christ Himself....Our Christ is not a blind Christ. He is the Christ with the seven eyes. Often, He transfuses His elements into us. At other times, He observes us like a flashlight, saying, "What are you doing? Are you fighting with your husband? Stop!" Have you not had this kind of experience? Day by day we experience this watching, observing, and transfusing Christ. This watching, observing, and transfusing take place through His eyes. His eyes are the Spirit, and the Spirit is simply Himself. If you do not believe it, you will miss the blessing.]

IV. THE SEVEN SPIRITS, SEVEN LAMPS, AND SEVEN EYES FOR GOD'S BUILDING

A. The Lamps and the Building

[The lamps in Exodus 25 are for the building up of the tabernacle, especially for the move in the tabernacle. Without light, it is impossible to move. The light is for the move, and the move is for God's building. The seven lamps, therefore, are for the building up of the tabernacle, God's dwelling place on earth.

The seven lamps in Zechariah 3 and 4 are for the recovery of God's building. The principle is the same in the rebuilding of the temple as it was in the building of the tabernacle. The same is true of the book of Revelation....Revelation begins with the seven local churches and it ends with the New Jerusalem. Although this book contains the judgment of God, this judgment is not the goal. Judgment is not for judgment; it is for God's building. The New Jerusalem, God's eternal dwelling place, issues out of this judgment.]

B. The Stone with Seven Eyes

Zechariah 3:9 says, "For behold the stone that I have laid before Joshua; upon one stone shall be seven eyes." In Revelation 5, the seven eyes are of the Lamb, but in Zechariah they are upon a stone.

[In Matthew 16:18 the Lord Jesus said, "And I say also unto thee, That thou art a stone, and upon this rock I will build my church" (Gk.). Here the Lord refers to Himself as the rock. In Matthew 21:42 He said, "Did ye never read in the scriptures, The stone which the builders rejected, the same is become the head of the corner: this is the Lord's doing, and it is marvelous in our eyes?" The stone referred to here is the very stone with the seven eyes in Zechariah 3:9.]

The verses show us clearly that the stone is just Christ Himself and that this stone is related to the building of God's house. Christ is the Lamb-stone with seven eyes for God's building.

C. Cleansing and Infusing

[Because your condition is not pure, some of you are still under the seven burning lamps. You are still involved with certain things that need to be searched and judged. Mainly we are not under the flaming lamps, but under the infusing

eyes. Are you under the searching lamps or the infusing eyes?
I am happy to be under the seven eyes. Suppose you are about
to quarrel with your wife. The seven eyes will immediately
become the seven lamps. At such a time, you need to repent
and say, "O Lord Jesus, forgive me. I am still in the flesh, and
I am so pitiful. Lord, thank You for Your blood. I confess my
failure and I apply Your blood to my situation." Whenever
you do this, the seven lamps turn into the seven eyes looking
at you, and immediately you are once again under His transfusing. Christ's essence and certain of His attributes are
transfused into your being.]

D. Purifying and Transforming

[First Peter 2:4 and 5 say, "To whom coming, as unto a
living stone, disallowed indeed of men, but chosen of God, and
precious, ye also, as living stones, are being built up a spiritual house" (Gk.). The way for us to become living stones is to
come to Him and to be seen by Him. As the Lord enlightens
and judges us, He looks at us, and His seven eyes transfuse
Himself into us. In this way we are transformed.]

[Even now, Christ's burning eyes are flaming over us to
enlighten, search, refine, and judge us, not that we might be
condemned, but that we might be purged, transformed, and
conformed to His image for God's building. The Lord's judgment is motivated by love. Because He loves the church, He
comes to search, enlighten, judge, refine, and purify us in
order to transform us into precious stones. Eventually, this
book [of Revelation] consummates in the New Jerusalem
which is built with precious materials. Where do these materials come from? They come from the seven eyes of Christ,
that is, from the life-giving, transforming Spirit.

In the book of Revelation the Spirit is not called the
life-giving Spirit or the transforming Spirit, but the seven
Spirits which are the seven burning, searching, judging
lamps. For the degraded church, the Spirit who gives life must
be the sevenfold burning Spirit. Today, the life-giving Spirit
must be the flaming Spirit, and the transforming Spirit must
be the searching and judging Spirit. His searching and judging

are His purifying and transforming. No one can be transformed into a precious stone without being searched by Him. How I look to the Lord that He would search us all. We are not here for doctrine and teaching; we are here under the enlightening of the pure Word and under the searching of the seven Spirits. We all need to be thoroughly searched, purified, and refined. If we are, we shall never be the same.]

SUMMARY

In the final book of the Bible, Revelation, the Spirit is called the "seven Spirits of God." This does not mean that there are seven different Spirits; rather this means that the Spirit of God is intensified seven times for God's move. The seven Spirits are also the seven lamps for shining and judging. They are also the seven eyes of the Lamb to observe and transfuse the believers with Christ's element. The seven Spirits which are the lamps and the eyes are for God's building. The sevenfold Spirit purifies, infuses and transforms the believers to make them precious stones fit for the New Jerusalem.

Questions

1. If there are not seven different spirits, why is the Spirit of God referred to as the seven Spirits?

2. What is the significance of the number seven?

3. Why does the Holy Spirit need to be intensified sevenfold?

4. Besides Revelation 4:5, where else are the seven lamps of the lampstand mentioned?

5. What is the function of the seven eyes?

6. How do Exodus 25, Zechariah 3 and 4, and Revelation 4 relate to God's building?

7. Who is the stone in Zechariah 3:9? What is the significance of the stone?

8. How do the seven lamps and seven eyes make us the precious stones?

9. What is the consummate issue of the sevenfold Spirit's work?

Quoted Portions
from (Lee/LSM) Publications

1. *Life-study of Revelation,* pp. 40-42, 213-214, 265, 778.

2. *The Spirit and the Body,* pp. 79-80.

3. *Life-study of Revelation,* pp. 780, 227.

THE ESSENTIAL AND ECONOMICAL SPIRIT

Scripture Reading

John 20:22; Acts 1:5,8; 2:1-4; Matt. 1:18-20;
Luke 1:35; 3:21-22; 1 Cor. 12:13; Acts 11:15-17

Outline

I. Two aspects of the Holy Spirit
  A. As breath for life
  B. As wind for power
  C. In the life and ministry of the Lord Jesus
II. Only one Spirit
III. The proper aim—outward power for inward life
IV. The baptism in the Holy Spirit
  A. Tongues not necessary evidence
  B. Experiencing the accomplished fact
    1. Accomplished once for all
    2. No need to analyze
    3. In relation to the Body
V. Experiencing the two aspects by calling on the Lord

Text

In Lesson Twenty-Two of the *Lesson Book on the Triune God and the Person and Work of Christ* we saw the matter of the essential and economical Spirit. Because this point is such a significant and crucial truth regarding the Spirit, we must consider it once again. We will also see more about the baptism in the Holy Spirit. Most Christians today are very confused about this matter.

I. TWO ASPECTS OF THE HOLY SPIRIT

[In chapter one of Acts the resurrected Christ charged His disciples to remain in Jerusalem for the baptism in the Holy Spirit: "For John indeed baptized in water, but you shall be

baptized in the Holy Spirit not many days from now" (Acts
1:5). In verse 8 He went on to say, "You shall receive power
when the Holy Spirit has come upon you." Here we see that
the baptism in the Holy Spirit is a matter of the Spirit
descending upon the disciples.]

A. As Breath for Life

[In Acts 1 the Lord talks about the disciples experiencing
the Holy Spirit coming upon them. But had the disciples not
received the Holy Spirit already? According to John 20, in the
evening of His resurrection day, the Lord appeared to His
disciples, breathed on them, and said to them, "Receive the
Holy Spirit" (v. 22). In this verse the Holy Spirit is likened to
breath. Breath is something inward, something related to the
life within us. In John 20:22, therefore, the disciples received
the Holy Spirit as breath for life.]

B. As Wind for Power

[The Lord's word to the disciples concerning the Holy
Spirit in chapter one of Acts was fulfilled in chapter two. On
the day of Pentecost "suddenly there came a noise out of
heaven like a rushing violent wind," and it filled the house
where the disciples were sitting. Then they were all filled
with the Holy Spirit (Acts 2:1-4). On the day of the Lord's
resurrection the disciples received the Holy Spirit as breath
for life. Then fifty days later, on the day of Pentecost, the Holy
Spirit came upon the disciples as a rushing mighty wind. We
can easily see the difference between breath and wind.
Breath is for life, and wind is for power. In John 20 and Acts 2
we have two symbols of the Holy Spirit: the breath for life
inwardly and the wind for power outwardly.]

C. In the Life and Ministry of the Lord Jesus

[With the Lord Jesus we also see these two aspects of the
Holy Spirit. First, the Lord was conceived of the Holy Spirit
(Luke 1:35; Matt. 1:18,20). Then at the age of thirty, when He
came forth to minister, the Holy Spirit descended upon Him,
and He was baptized in the Holy Spirit (Luke 3:21-22). The

Lord's being conceived of the Spirit was a matter of the Spirit essentially, but His being baptized in the Holy Spirit was a matter of the Spirit descending upon Him economically. Hence, the Holy Spirit for the Lord's conception was essential, whereas the Holy Spirit for His ministry was economical.]

II. ONLY ONE SPIRIT

[It is important for us to differentiate these two aspects of the Spirit, for then we shall understand the Gospels and Acts in the right way. Otherwise, we shall be confused.]

On one point, however, we must be very clear: [We should not think that there are two Spirits or that the Spirit can somehow be divided. On the contrary, there is one Spirit. Yet there are the two aspects of the Spirit, one aspect for essence and another aspect for economy. The first aspect of the Spirit is essential; the second aspect is economical. Today in our experience we have both aspects of the Holy Spirit. We have both the essential Spirit and the economical Spirit.]

III. THE PROPER AIM—
OUTWARD POWER FOR INWARD LIFE

We must also be clear that the outward, economical aspect is not the aim; the economical is for the essential. [The outward aspect of power is always for the sake of the inward aspect of life. It is by the inward that God's desire, God's central aim is fulfilled. The outward aspect is the *means* of accomplishing the inward aspect. In 1 Corinthians 12:13, we have these two aspects mentioned in the proper order. We were "baptized" first, and we were made to "drink" second. After we have been baptized in the Spirit into one Body, we must drink of the Spirit that we may grow in life and be built up in the Body. To be baptized in the Holy Spirit is to be put into Him, just as to be baptized in water is to be put into it. But to drink of the Holy Spirit is to take Him into us just as to drink water is to take it into us. Baptism is outward and drinking is inward. The outward baptism is for the inward drinking.]

IV. THE BAPTISM IN THE HOLY SPIRIT

[The outward aspect of the Holy Spirit's work is mostly included in the baptism in the Holy Spirit. There are five historical cases of the outpouring of the Spirit recorded in Acts. Only two are called the baptism in the Holy Spirit: the outpouring at the Day of Pentecost in Acts 2 for the Jewish believers and the outpouring in the house of Cornelius in Acts 10 for the Gentile believers. Acts 1:5 and 11:15-17 verify this fact. In these two instances, Christ as the Head baptized the Jewish and Gentile parts of His Body in the Holy Spirit once and for all. By so doing, He has fully accomplished the baptism in the Holy Spirit upon His entire Body.]

[The other three, the cases of the Samaritan believers, Saul of Tarsus, and the twelve believers in Ephesus, are all considered extraordinary, needing some members of the Body of Christ to identify them with the Body by the laying on of hands. Besides these five cases, in many cases of conversion, such as the three thousand (2:41), the five thousand (4:4), the Ethiopian eunuch (8:36, 38-39a), the many who believed in Antioch (11:20-21, 24), the many cases in chapters thirteen and fourteen under Paul's preaching ministry, Lydia in Philippi (16:14-15), the jailer in Philippi (16:33), the believers in Thessalonica (17:4), the believers in Berea (17:10-12), the believers in Athens (17:34), the ruler of the synagogue and many other believers in Corinth (18:8), and the believers in Ephesus (19:18-19), there is no mention of the believers' receiving the Holy Spirit economically—the Holy Spirit's falling upon the believers—because in all these cases the believers were brought into the Body of Christ through their believing in a normal way, and they had no particular reason for some member of the Body of Christ to bring them into the identification with the Body by the laying on of hands. According to the principle of God's New Testament economy, they all should have received the Holy Spirit essentially for life and economically for power in a normal way through their believing into Christ.]

A. Tongues Not Necessary Evidence

[Some Christians always insist that speaking in tongues is a necessary manifestation (evidence) of the baptism in the Holy Spirit. But with two of the five cases in Acts—the Samaritans and Saul of Tarsus—nothing is mentioned about speaking in tongues. Students of the Scripture admit that many times what God *does not* mention is more meaningful than what He *does* mention. With two of these five cases, no specific manifestation is mentioned. This is an indication that a tongue is not the only or the necessary manifestation of the baptism in the Holy Spirit. Even with the other cases, there is no proof that all the believers spoke in tongues.]

The "tongues" spoken in Acts 2:4 [were dialects (vv. 6, 8). The disciples were Galileans (v. 7), yet they spoke the different foreign dialects of the attendants who came from various parts of the world. This is strong proof that tongue-speaking must be an understandable language, not merely a voice or sound uttered by the tongue.] Based on this we must say that nearly all of today's so called tongue-speaking is not according to the truth of the Bible.

B. Experiencing the Accomplished Fact

1. Accomplished Once for All

We have given many lessons [in the effort to point out what the Triune God has accomplished. The Triune God in the Son became flesh. That was the incarnation. The incarnation has been accomplished once for all, and there is no need for it to be repeated. Likewise, Christ was crucified and died once for all. Furthermore, He was resurrected, He breathed Himself as the life-giving Spirit into His disciples, He ascended, and He poured out Himself as the all-inclusive Spirit once for all. Christ has accomplished all these things, and He has accomplished them once for all. Now all these matters are included in the Lord's name. Therefore, when we call on the name of the Lord Jesus, we receive all these things.]

2. No Need to Analyze

[There is no need for us to analyze what we receive through calling on the name of the Lord Jesus. We should not ask ourselves, "Have I received the essential Spirit? Has the economical Spirit fallen upon me? Perhaps I have the essential Spirit within me, but I wonder if I have the economical Spirit. Maybe the economical Spirit will leave me, although the essential Spirit will not leave. If the economical Spirit leaves, when will He come back?" It is not a healthy practice to analyze these matters in this way.]

There is also [no need for us to seek feelings, manifestations of signs. We should never trust in these things. If we seek them, we have an evil heart of unbelief. We are trying to prove or tempt the Lord.]

3. In Relation to the Body

The Word of God tells us that the baptism in the Holy Spirit is an accomplished fact for us to apply. We simply need to believe this and enjoy it. There are, however, some conditions.

[We must be right with the Body of Christ and stand in it. Since the baptism in the Holy Spirit has been accomplished upon the Body of Christ and still exists upon it, we must be properly related to the Body and maintain this proper relationship with the Body in order to be one with it. Of course, we ourselves must get right with the Lord. Any sin, anything wrong between us and God, must be thoroughly dealt with through the cleansing of the blood of Christ. Nothing between the Lord and us should be allowed to remain. But we must also get right with the Body of Christ. Anything that frustrates, distracts, or separates us from the Body must be fully dealt with and real oneness and harmony maintained with the Body and its members.]

V. EXPERIENCING THE TWO ASPECTS BY CALLING ON THE LORD

[Today we need to learn to call upon the name of the Lord. I am heavily burdened to impress you with the need of calling. Throughout the centuries, Satan has shut the mouths of so many Christians. If you call on the name of the Lord Jesus all day long, you will be saturated, permeated, and soaked with the Spirit, and the power poured out from on high will be your portion. There is no need for me to convince you of this. Check your past experience. Often when you found yourself in trouble, you called on the name of the Lord. We all have some amount of experience. Usually we did not call on the Lord. We simply did not like calling on His name. Therefore, the Lord sent us some difficulty to help us or even force us to call on Him. When the troubles came, we spontaneously called out, "O Lord Jesus." Perhaps we did not call in a very pleasant way. Nevertheless, we called and we received breath, strengthening, and refreshment. I want to impress you that the secret of experiencing the inward aspect and the outward aspect of this wonderful Spirit is simply to call again and again. After you call, you will pray. Then you will call more and pray more. Eventually, it will be difficult to tell whether you are experiencing the inward aspect or the outward aspect. Then you will be filled with refreshment, and outwardly you will be released. You will have the power, the boldness, the assurance, and the faith to speak strongly. You will not have any doubts whatever. The way to experience this wonderful Spirit is by calling on the name of the Lord Jesus. Be simple and call on the name of the Lord.]

SUMMARY

There are two aspects of the Spirit: essential and economical. The essential is for life inwardly, and the economical is for power outwardly. The outward power is for the inward life. The outward aspect is mostly included in the baptism in the Holy Spirit, which was accomplished upon the Body once for all on the Day of Pentecost and in the house of Cornelius. We received the Holy Spirit essentially and economically in a normal way through our believing into Christ. We do not need to speak in tongues or seek feelings or signs. We can experience both aspects simply by calling on the Lord.

Questions

1. What are the two aspects of the Holy Spirit? How do they relate to each other?

2. How can we see the two aspects of the Spirit in the life and ministry of the Lord Jesus.

3. Name the five historical cases of the outpouring of the Spirit recorded in Acts. How do the first two cases differ from the other three?

4. What is the normal way for a believer to receive the Spirit essentially and economically?

5. What is a strong proof showing that the tongue-speaking in Acts was an understandable language?

6. What is a simple way to experience the inward and outward aspect of the Spirit?

Quoted Portions
from (Lee/LSM) Publications

1. *Life-study of Mark,* pp. 565-567.

2. *Life-study of Acts,* p. 52.

3. *Life-study of Mark,* p. 570.

4. *The Baptism in the Holy Spirit,* pp. 5-6.

5. *Life-study of Acts,* p. 250.

6. *The Baptism in the Holy Spirit,* p. 11.

7. *Life-study of Acts,* pp. 60-61, 260-261.

8. *The Baptism in the Holy Spirit,* pp. 15, 14.

9. *The Spirit and the Body,* pp. 45-46.

THE SPIRIT'S WORK IN THE BELIEVERS (1) — REGENERATION

Scripture Reading

John 3:3-6; Eph. 2:1; 1 Cor. 6:17; Rom. 8:16;
Jer. 17:9; 13:23; Rom. 7:18; Col. 1:12-13; Acts 11:15-17

Outline

I. Regeneration
   A. Born of the Spirit
   B. Born again
   C. The way to be regenerated
II. The need of regeneration
   A. Because we are corrupted
   B. Because we lack God's life
III. Regeneration versus the natural concept
   A. Receiving the life and nature of God
   B. Not outward decoration
   C. Living as sons of God
IV. The constant receiving of the Spirit

Text

I. REGENERATION

In the next five lessons we will see some major aspects of the Spirit's work in the believers. The Spirit's work is mainly *within* the believers; it is for the dispensing of God into man. Regeneration is the reality and initiation of the divine dispensing. As the Spirit, God dispenses His life and nature into our being. Only by being the Spirit is God able to regenerate us.

A. Born of the Spirit

[According to the Bible, to be regenerated is to be born of the Spirit (John 3:3-6). Before regeneration our spirit was dead. "And you, being dead in your offenses and sins" (Eph. 2:1). But at the time we believed, God's Spirit came into us and mingled with our spirit (1 Cor. 6:17; Rom. 8:16). Thus, our spirit obtained God's life and was made alive. Whereas our parents gave us our natural birth, God's Spirit has given us our spiritual birth.]

B. Born Again

[Regeneration also means to be born again or born anew. Originally we were born of our parents, but now we are born once more, this time of God. The Bible calls this experience being born again. When we were born of our parents, we obtained human life. When we were born of God, we obtained God's divine life.]

C. The Way to be Regenerated

[How can God's Spirit enter into man's spirit? When man hears the Gospel or reads the word of the Scripture, God's Spirit works in him and causes him to feel that he has sinned and is corrupted; hence, he is reproved for sin and righteousness and judgment (John 16:8). When man sees himself as a sinner, recognizes his corruption, and is willing to repent, then God's Spirit causes him to see that the Lord Jesus is his Savior, and that He died on the cross to shed His blood for the remission of sin. At this moment, he automatically believes in the Lord and receives Him as his Savior. Once he receives the Lord as his Savior, God's Spirit enters into his spirit and puts God's life in it, causing him to be regenerated.]

II. THE NEED OF REGENERATION

A. Because We Are Corrupted

[We need to be regenerated because of two conditions. From the negative side, we need to be regenerated because our life has been corrupted and has become evil, and cannot be improved from evil to good. "The heart is deceitful above all things, and desperately wicked: who can know it?" (Jer. 17:9). "Can the Ethiopian change his skin, or the leopard his spots? Then may ye also do good, that are accustomed to do evil" (Jer. 13:23). "For I know that in me, that is in my flesh, nothing good dwells" (Rom. 7:18).]

B. Because We Lack God's Life

[From the positive side, however, we need to be regenerated because we do not have the life of God. Of all God's creation, man has the highest development of life. No plant or animal has a higher life than man. Yet man, the highest created life, needs to receive another life for his completion. He needs the uncreated, eternal life of God. When Adam was created, he obtained only created life; he did not at that time obtain God's uncreated life. Likewise, when we were born of our parents, we obtained only the natural, created human life. That birth gave us an entrance into the human kingdom. But for us to enter the kingdom of God, we must have another birth from another source. We must be born of God. By our first birth we were born into the kingdom of darkness, but by our second birth we are transferred into the kingdom of the Son of His love (Col. 1:13).

God's purpose is that we may obtain His own uncreated life and be transformed by this life into His image to be like Him. Even if our human life had not been corrupted by the fall of man in Genesis 3, we would still need to be regenerated. In Genesis 1 and 2, Adam was without sin, yet he was void of God's life. Thus, God placed him before the tree of life that he might receive the life of God and be regenerated. God's purpose in creating man is not merely to obtain a sinless man, but even more to have a God-man, one who has God's own life and nature.]

III. REGENERATION
VERSUS THE NATURAL CONCEPT

A. Receiving the Life and Nature of God

[It is the greatest wonder in the entire universe that human beings could be begotten of God, and sinners could be made children of God! Through such an amazing divine birth we have received the divine life, which is the eternal life (1 John 1:2), as the divine seed sown into our being.]

[Suppose a dog could be born of its master and receive its master's life and nature. Such an event would surely catch the attention of the news media. Would it not be a great miracle for the life and nature of a human being to be imparted to a dog and to make that dog a man-dog? Such a dog would not simply be washed, decorated, and beautified. It would actually have the life and nature of a human being. As astounding as it may seem, through regeneration we have received the life and nature of God.]

B. Not Outward Decoration

[This understanding of regeneration shatters the natural concept. Using the illustration of a dog receiving a human life, we see that the natural concept is merely that a dog can be cleansed and beautified. In principle, many Christians are occupied with cleansing people and beautifying them, instead of helping them receive the divine life and nature through regeneration. God's way is not merely to wash us, beautify us, and decorate us outwardly. His intention in His economy is to regenerate us, to cause us to be sons of God born of Him. This matter is unspeakably great.

There is no doubt that God's salvation includes cleansing by the redeeming blood of Christ. In a very real sense, we, the saved ones, have been cleansed by God. Being cleansed, however, is not the highlight of God's salvation. The highlight is that God has regenerated us, that He has actually imparted His life and nature into us to make us His sons. Now we are not God's sons-in-law—we are the sons of God in life. Certainly there is no greater wonder in the whole universe than that sinful men by being regenerated can become sons of God. Many today are seeking wonders and miracles. But they do not realize that there is no greater miracle than regeneration. By regeneration fallen people become sons of God. In His salvation God has made us, fallen sinners, His divine sons.]

C. Living as Sons of God

[Not many Christians realize that they are sons of God and that God wants them to live the life of a son of God. After they are saved, most Christians try to improve themselves or to do something to please God. In their efforts to improve the natural man or to do something to please God, the vast majority of the Lord's people are missing the mark of God's economy. God's salvation is for His economy, and His economy is not a matter of ethics. Rather, by His salvation according to His economy, God has regenerated us by the divine life that we may be His sons and live as sons of God. God's goal is not simply that we improve our behavior and thereby do good instead of evil. It is not God's purpose merely to have a number of good people. God's desire is that we live as sons of God. God wants us not simply to be cleansed. He wants us to live as sons of God. If we would do this, we need to receive the Spirit of God. We have been born of the Spirit to receive the Spirit.]

IV. THE CONSTANT RECEIVING OF THE SPIRIT

[Galatians 3:5 says, "He therefore Who is supplying to you the Spirit and doing works of power among you, is it by the works of law or by the hearing of faith?" This verse indicates that God continues to supply us the Spirit. We may use electricity as an illustration. After electricity has been installed in a building, electricity is supplied continually to the building. Likewise, after God regenerated us by His Spirit to make us His sons, He has been continually supplying to us the Spirit. Nothing is more crucial than the constant receiving of the Spirit.]

Instead of trying to behave religiously we should pray, ["Lord Jesus, I open myself to You. I thank You that I have been born of God, born of the all-inclusive Spirit. Lord, this Spirit is still transmitting something of You into my being. I thank You, Lord, for this marvelous transmission."] Then we will be the sons of God living by and enjoying the divine dispensing of the Triune God. Hallelujah for regeneration!

SUMMARY

Regeneration is the initiation of the divine dispensing. When God's Spirit enters into a person, his spirit is made alive; he is born of the Spirit. This is to be born again. It is a

spiritual birth in addition to our natural birth. Man needs
regeneration not only because he has been corrupted but even
the more because he lacks God's life. Regeneration is entirely
different from the natural concept of outwardly decorating
people. Regeneration causes people to receive the very life
and nature of God and makes them sons of God. The believers
should continue to live by this life which is transmitted by the
Spirit.

Questions

1. What happens to man's spirit at regeneration?

2. Why does the Bible refer to regeneration as being "born
   again"?

3. What are the two aspects of man's need of regeneration?

4. How does regeneration relate to God's purpose?

5. How can we see from Genesis that Adam needed regeneration even before he sinned?

6. What is the natural or religious concept about changing a
   person? How is regeneration different?

Quoted Portions
from (Lee/LSM) Publications

1. *What is Regeneration?*, p. 6.

2. *The Knowledge of Life,* pp. 26-27.

3. *What is Regeneration?*, pp. 7-8.

4. *Life-study of First John,* pp. 25, 214.

5. *Life-study of Galatians,* pp. 32, 279-280, 283-284.

Lesson Eight

THE SPIRIT'S WORK IN THE BELIEVERS (2) — SANCTIFICATION

Scripture Reading

2 Thes. 2:13; 1 Pet. 1:1-2; Rom. 6:19; 8:2, 10;
John 20:22; 1 Thes. 5:23; John 6:63; 17:17

Outline

I. Sanctification
II. The two aspects of sanctification
   A. Before justification
   B. After justification
     1. Positional sanctification
     2. Dispositional sanctification
III. Sanctification by the Word and the Spirit

Text

I. SANCTIFICATION

Sanctification is the process by which something is made holy. Many people would say that this means that we should not sin and that we should stay away from evil things. That, however, is only a small part of sanctification.

[God's eternal purpose is to work Himself into us that He may be thoroughly mingled with us and expressed through us. When God is born into us, He begins this mingling process. But this is only the start! There must be the growth. If we have the birth, but not the growth, we could never enjoy the birthright. God is born into our spirit, which is the very center of our being. Then His desire is to spread from our spirit to transform all the parts of the soul, and eventually to transfigure our physical body. By this process our whole being will be saturated and permeated with the essence of God Himself. This is the real holiness and the real sanctification: to be completely mingled with God.]

Second Thessalonians 2:13 says, "God chose you from the beginning unto salvation in sanctification of the Spirit and belief of the truth." [The Spirit is sanctifying the believers, separating them entirely for God's eternal purpose; from the day we first heard the gospel the sanctifying Spirit sanctifies us by dispensing the Triune God into us.]

II. THE TWO ASPECTS OF SANCTIFICATION

[The sanctification of the Spirit is of two aspects: the sanctification of the Spirit before justification, the first aspect, and the sanctification of the Spirit after justification, the second aspect. With the second aspect of the Spirit's sanctification there are two sides—the positional side and the dispositional side. After God justifies us and regenerates us, immediately the sanctifying Spirit continues His separating work upon us and within us. First, the sanctifying Spirit separates us positionally from things that are common and worldly. This positional sanctification is objective. Simultaneously, the sanctifying Spirit also begins to sanctify us dispositionally. This means that the Spirit is sanctifying our disposition. This is the subjective side of the sanctifying work of the Holy Spirit. The subjective sanctification is what we mean by the work of transformation. Subjective sanctification involves the transformation of our disposition and our inward parts. Therefore, this transformation of our disposition is the dispositional sanctification of the Spirit.]

A. Before Justification

First Peter 1:1-2 says that we were chosen "according to the foreknowledge of God the Father, in sanctification of the Spirit, unto obedience and sprinkling of the blood of Jesus Christ."

[Peter says that sanctification comes after the Father's selection and before Christ's redemption. According to this verse, the sanctification of the Spirit is unto the obedience and sprinkling of the blood of Christ. Surely, this indicates that the sanctification of the Spirit precedes the redemption of Christ....

In eternity past God selected us. But how could this selection be applied to us? In order for it to be applied, there is the need of the Spirit's application. We all can testify of this from our experience. We were wandering on earth, perhaps as those who never had a thought concerning God. But one day the "wind" of the Spirit "blew" us to a place where we heard the preaching of the gospel. While we were listening to the preaching of the gospel, faith was infused into us. In this way God's selection was applied to us. The next thing to be applied was the redemption of Christ. In this sense the sanctification of the Spirit preceded our experience of Christ's redemption.]

[I can use my own experience to illustrate this aspect of the Spirit's sanctification. I was born into the religion of Christianity, but, of course, I was not born into Christ. As a young person, I became quite rebellious, having seen some things in Christianity that I did not agree with.

But one day, at the age of nineteen, I was arrested by the sanctifying Spirit. A young woman evangelist came to our town, and out of curiosity I went to listen to her. As I sat in the meeting, the Spirit asked me, "What are you doing here? I have been pursuing you for a long time, and now is the time for Me to catch you." I was indeed caught for the Lord at that time. I repented and I began to obey Christ and accept what He did. No doubt, at the same time I received the sprinkling of the blood of Christ, and I experienced the first aspect of the sanctifying work of the Spirit. From that time onward, the Spirit has been continually sanctifying me. Even now this sanctifying work, the second aspect of the Spirit's sanctification, is still going on.

The sanctifying work of the Spirit began before God's justification and it continues afterward. Before justification, we are separated unto obedience and sprinkling of the blood of Christ.]

B. After Justification

1. Positional Sanctification

[In order for us to be holy, we first need to be separated unto God positionally. With respect to our family, neighbors, colleagues, and friends, we need to be separated.] This does not necessarily mean to be separated physically, but it means that we are different in the way we think, the things we speak, and the things we do.

Romans 6:19 says, "I speak humanly because of the weakness of your flesh. For as you presented your members as slaves to uncleanness and lawlessness unto lawlessness, so now present your members as slaves to righteousness unto sanctification."

[Many Christians, however, are saved, but not separated. Normally, once a person is saved, he should also be separated. This is the reason a believer is called a saint. Consider the majority of Christians today. They are virtually the same as the worldly people. With them, there is no separation. Many of their relatives and friends do not even know that they are Christians. But to be holy is to be separated unto God. This, of course, is a matter of position.]

[Admittedly, separation is not a very deep matter; it is merely positional. But do not think that position is unimportant. It means a great deal. We have a position as saints, as separated ones, and we need to keep it.]

2. Dispositional Sanctification

[In subjective sanctification we are saturated with God dispositionally. Separation can take place rather easily and in a very short time. But to be saturated dispositionally takes a long time. If we are faithful to the Lord, we shall be saturated with the nature of God day after day. God intends to saturate us with Himself, and we need to soak up God in our being. This requires time. This is the process of being made holy.]

[In order to accomplish this God has been processed into the available Spirit of life (Rom. 8:2). Before being processed He was not available to perform this subjective work of sanctification. Before He was processed He was able to create the world, but He was unable to enter into His creature. Although He could do many things outside of us, He could not come into us until He had passed through the complete process of incarnation, crucifixion, and resurrection. Since being processed, He has become and still is the available Spirit of life. Now, like the air for breathing (John 20:22), it is so easy for Him to enter into us. As the available Spirit of life, God has come into our spirit, making it life. Since Christ, the life-giving Spirit, is in us, our spirit is life because of righteousness (Rom. 8:10). The Lord has made our spirit life by regeneration. Now, as the Spirit of life in our spirit, He is spreading Himself from our spirit into our soul—into our mind, emotion, and will. Eventually, He will even expand into our mortal body. In such a way God saturates us with Himself. This saturation is called sanctification. Through this saturation God works Himself with His holy nature into our entire being, into our spirit, soul, and body (1 Thes. 5:23). Thus, our whole being will be fully permeated, sanctified, with His holy nature. We are presently undergoing this process of sanctification.]

III. SANCTIFICATION BY THE WORD AND THE SPIRIT

This sanctification takes place by the Word, which is truth, and by the Spirit, which is the Spirit of truth. In the Gospel of John the Word and the Spirit are mentioned often. In 6:63 the Lord said, "The words I speak unto you are spirit and are life." In 17:17 He prayed, "Sanctify them in the truth; Your word is truth."

[Actually, the Word and the Spirit are one. I thank the Lord that so many of us have come back to the Word and are getting into the Word every day. As we come to the Word every morning, outwardly we touch the Word, but inwardly the Spirit touches us. By the Word and by the Spirit, both of which are the reality, we are sanctified.]

[Suppose the young people touch the Word with the Spirit in morning watch and then go to school. Throughout the day at school, this word of truth will work within them to separate them and make them different from their classmates in their behavior, actions, work, thoughts, and feelings. Something is working within them to sanctify them, to make them holy.

By taking the Word in this way, we have the clear conviction that something of the Lord has been wrought into us. This is not the mere knowledge of the Bible or of things concerning the Lord. It is the reality of the Triune God living, moving, working, and separating us. This makes us different from the worldly people. I can tell by the faces of the young people that they are graced by the Lord's presence. What a blessing! Every morning we can touch the living Word and have the divine reality infused into our being. In this way the Triune God is transfused into us.]

SUMMARY

After regenerating our spirit, God desires to saturate our entire being with Himself. This is the Spirit's work of sanctification. The sanctification of the Spirit is of two aspects: before justification and after justification. Before justification, the Spirit works to bring us to repentance. After we repent and are justified, the Spirit continues to sanctify us on two sides, positionally and dispositionally. A practical way to be sanctified is by being touched by the Spirit in the Word.

Questions

1. Why do we say that sanctification is more than just not sinning?

2. What are the two aspects of sanctification? Briefly explain the two aspects.

3. What are the two sides of sanctification after justification? Briefly explain the two sides.

4. How is it that God the Creator can enter into man and saturate his whole being?

5. What verse in the Gospel of John tells us that the Word can sanctify us?

Quoted Portions
from (Lee/LSM) Publications

1. *God's Purpose for the Church,* p. 6.

2. *1985 Winter Training Message Abstracts,* p. 6.

3. *Life-study of First Peter,* pp. 42-43, 32-33, 19-20.

4. *Life-study of Ephesians,* pp. 28, 30.

5. *Life-study of Romans,* p. 204.

6. *Truth Messages,* pp. 54, 42.

THE SPIRIT'S WORK IN THE BELIEVERS (3)—
TRANSFORMATION

Scripture Reading

2 Cor. 3:18; Rom. 12:2

Outline

I. Transformation
  A. The result of sanctification
  B. A metabolic change
    1. Discharging the old element and adding the new
    2. By taking in the all-inclusive Spirit
II. The way to be transformed
  A. Not conformed but transformed by the renewing of the mind
  B. Beholding and reflecting the Lord

Text

I. TRANSFORMATION

A. The Result of Sanctification

In the previous lesson we saw the matter of sanctification, the imparting of the divine life into our entire being. [When life is imparted into us, the result is transformation. It is similar to a chemical reaction caused by one element being added to another. The divine life brought into us through sanctification is a divine chemical element. When this element is imparted into our being, there is a reaction, and that reaction is transformation. Transformation means to change our nature, essence, appearance, tastes, and our whole being. Transformation is not outward change, correction, or adjustment; it is altogether an inward, metabolic change of our being.]

B. A Metabolic Change

1. Discharging the Old Element
and Adding the New

[In the physical body metabolism refers to the processes in cells by which old materials are discharged and new are added. This change, applied to the soul, is called in the New Testament transformation (2 Cor. 3:18; Rom. 12:2). To apply makeup may result in a change in appearance, but it is merely an outward, not a metabolic, change. To have a better skin color because of an improved diet, on the other hand, is the result of a metabolic process. New elements are organically assimilated by the body, replacing the old. Transformation is a change in life, not merely in appearance. The divine element is added to us; this discharges the old human element. This organic change takes place in our soul.]

2. By Taking in the All-Inclusive Spirit

[Our spirit, then, needs regeneration; our soul, transformation. In all the churches the saints should be concerned about this metabolic change in life through the spreading of the divine Spirit.] [This Spirit is the very essence and element of the Lord Jesus. After you were saved, He began to impart His element into you. Day by day, as you open yourself and give Him opportunity, He will impart His element into you. Doctrines are not the element. Only Christ Himself, the all-inclusive, life-giving Spirit is the element. Such a Christ as the all-inclusive Spirit is imparting Himself into your spirit, and from your spirit into your whole being. He will spread into your heart, mind, emotion, and will. This element of Christ is truly a transforming element. Once this element comes into you, something happens. For example, after mothers feed their children, the food is digested and assimilated by the children. The element of the food enters the children's blood, and then it penetrates their cells and organic tissues, causing them to grow.]

In the same way, [we simply need to open ourselves continually and say to the Lord, "O Lord Jesus! Come in, Lord Jesus! Fill me up, Lord Jesus!" Open yourself and let Christ fill you. If you are faithful to receive Him in a constant and thorough way, He will spread into your inner being. By the proper digestion and assimilation, you will be saturated by all the nourishing elements of Christ.]

II. THE WAY TO BE TRANSFORMED

A. Not Conformed but Transformed by the Renewing of the Mind

Romans 12:2 says, "Do not be conformed to this age, but be transformed by the renewing of the mind." [If we are occupied by the things of this age, our mind can never be renewed. This is why many Christians who are really saved cannot understand spiritual things. They have become too modern. We have to give up this modern age. If we are conformed to this age, we can never be transformed by the renewing of the mind.

Since the mind is a part of the soul, it is in the soul that transformation takes place. We have been regenerated in the spirit, but now the problem is the soul....In our spirit we are entirely different from the people of the world, but I am afraid that in our mind, will, and emotion we are still exactly the same. Regeneration has been accomplished in our spirit, but after regeneration, we still need the transformation in the soul.

Let us illustrate this by a few instances. What about our clothing? Many who are saved are just like the people of the world in their thinking about fashion. They dress in conformity to this modern age. They think that as long as it is not sinful, it is quite all right, but this is merely the human thought and the natural concept. If they would be transformed by the renewing of their mind, their thoughts about their manner of dress would change.

And what about our spending? Has the way we use our money been changed? I know the story of many Christians. After they are saved, they continue to use their money in much the same way as those in the world. Not until they love the Lord more and give the Lord more ground to work within them will they be transformed in their way of spending money.

In the same way, there are many young brothers studying in the colleges who have the same thoughts about their studies and their degrees as other worldly young people. But if they would give ground to the Lord and be transformed in the soul by the renewing of their mind, their mind would be changed about these matters. This does not mean that they would give up their studies, but that their thoughts and concepts about their studies would be entirely different. They would have another point of view from which to evaluate their studies and their degrees.

There should be a change in our thoughts towards almost everything. What is this change in our thoughts? It is the transformation of our soul by the renewing of our mind. We have Christ as life within our spirit, but now we need Christ to spread into the inward parts of the soul and saturate them with Himself. This will transform our soul into His very image. The image of Christ will then be reflected in our thoughts. In whatever we think and consider, our renewed mind will express the glorious image of Christ. The understanding of our mind will then be spiritual.]

B. Beholding and Reflecting the Lord

Second Corinthians 3:18 tells us how we can be transformed: "And we all with unveiled face, beholding and reflecting as a mirror the glory of the Lord, are being transformed into the same image from glory to glory, even as from the Lord Spirit."

[As we behold and reflect as a mirror the glory of the Lord, we are transformed into the Lord's image from one stage of glory to another. When a mirror beholds anything, it reflects what it beholds. But if a mirror is veiled, its face is not open; even if it beholds an object, it cannot reflect it. If we are an open mirror, we will reflect Christ by beholding Him. This is the process of transformation. The Lord is the Spirit transforming us within. Although we are so natural and even sinful, the Spirit transforms our natural image into His glorious image.]

[If we are still veiled in some way, we shall be like a camera with the lens covered. No light will be able to penetrate our inner being. If we want to be unveiled, we need to say to the Lord, "Lord, take away anything that is covering me. Lord, remove my veils. Take away any opinions that are veils to me. Lord, I want to be completely open, absolutely unveiled." Then with an unveiled face we shall behold and reflect the glory of the Lord and be transformed into His image from glory to glory.

Today the glory is the resurrected Christ, and this Christ is the Spirit. This means that the Lord as the glory is the Spirit living in us and dwelling in our spirit. Now that we have the Spirit indwelling our spirit, we need to exercise our spirit more and more by praying, reading the Word, and calling on the name of the Lord. The more we exercise our spirit with an unveiled face, the more we shall behold the Lord. As we are gazing on Him, we shall also reflect Him. While we are beholding and reflecting Him in this way, His element, His essence, will be added into our being. This new element will replace and discharge the element of our old, natural life. Then we shall experience transformation, a metabolic change. We shall be transformed into the Lord's image.]

SUMMARY

Transformation is the change or reaction in our being that results from the divine life being imparted into us. This is not just an outward change but a change in life, a metabolic change in our soul. When we open to the Lord, Christ as the Spirit imparts Himself into us as the transforming element. We should not be conformed to this modern age, but be transformed by the renewing of the mind. By beholding and reflecting the Lord with an unveiled face, we will be transformed into His image.

Questions

1. How does transformation relate to sanctification?

2. Briefly describe how a chemical reaction can illustrate the process of transformation.

3. What is the difference between a metabolic change and a mere outward change in appearance? Relate this to our transformation.

4. What are the two verses in the New Testament that tell us how we can be transformed?

Quoted Portions
from (Lee/LSM) Publications

1. *The Spirit and the Body,* pp. 69-70.

2. *The Completing Ministry of Paul,* p. 66.

3. *The Kingdom,* pp. 157-159.

4. *The Economy of God,* pp. 82-83, 25.

5. *Life-study of Second Corinthians,* pp. 213-214.

Lesson Ten

THE SPIRIT'S WORK IN THE BELIEVERS (4)— THE ANOINTING, SEALING, AND PLEDGING

Scripture Reading

2 Cor. 1:21-22; 1 John 2:27; Eph. 1:11, 13-14

Outline

I. The anointing
   A. The moving of the Spirit in us
   B. Adding the diving element
II. The sealing
   A. Indicating ownership
   B. Bearing the image of God
III. The pledging
   A. A sample and a foretaste
   B. Given for our enjoyment
IV. A mutual inheritance

Text

In this lesson we shall consider some symbols that the New Testament uses to describe the work of the Spirit in us. Second Corinthians 1:21-22 says, "But He who firmly attaches us with you unto Christ and has anointed us is God, Who has also sealed us and given the pledge of the Spirit in our hearts." In these verses we see the Spirit as the anointing, as the seal, and as the pledge.

I. THE ANOINTING

A. The Moving of the Spirit in Us

First John 2:27 says, "The anointing which you received from Him abides in you, and you have no need that anyone should teach you; but as His anointing teaches you concerning all things."

[The anointing is very mysterious, but it is also real and

experiential. Instead of using the noun "ointment," John uses the verbal noun "anointing." This word refers to the moving of the all-inclusive Spirit within us.] [This Spirit is the fulfillment of the type of the compound ointment revealed in Exodus 30. In this compound ointment there are a number of different elements which are the ingredients of the ointment. Just as paint may have a number of different elements, so the anointing Spirit also has different elements.] These elements include divinity, humanity, the effectiveness of Christ's death, the power of His resurrection, and the ability to bear responsibility.

B. Adding the Divine Element

[When the Triune God reaches us today, He comes as the Spirit. The moving of this Spirit is the anointing within (1 John 2:27). The Triune God dwells in us as the all-inclusive, compound, life-giving Spirit, and this Spirit is the ointment moving within....He is not dormant within us; rather, He is living, moving, acting. This is the anointing, which is the Triune God as the all-inclusive Spirit moving in us to saturate us with God's essence.]

[This anointing adds to us the very essence of God, the divine element. This is similar to the process of painting a table. As you paint the table, the element of the paint is added to the table. Likewise, as the ointment runs through us, it brings the divine element into us. In the Lord's recovery we have the assurance that day by day something is running through us, doing an inward "painting" work. The more this ointment moves, the more it paints us with the divine element. Hallelujah, the divine element is being added to us in the Lord's recovery! This is not a matter of teaching. Something is running over us and through us, and the divine element is being accumulated within us. The more we enjoy the flowing of the inner life and the more we enjoy the Lord together in the meetings, the more we have God within us. Although we may still feel that we are weak, we nevertheless have God within, for the anointing is constantly adding the divine element into our being.]

II. THE SEALING

[After the anointing comes the sealing. The sealing is rather easy to understand. Any kind of painting is also a sealing.]

A. Indicating Ownership

Ephesians 1:13-14 says, "You were sealed with the Holy Spirit of the promise...unto the redemption of the acquired possession." [To be sealed with the Holy Spirit means to be marked with the Holy Spirit as a living seal. We have been made God's inheritance (v. 11). At the time we were saved, God put His Holy Spirit into us as a seal to mark us out, indicating that we belong to God. The Holy Spirit, who is God Himself entering into us, causes us to bear God's image signified by the seal, thus making us like God. Suppose a brother puts a seal on his Bible. When he does so, his Bible bears the image of the seal. This seal indicates that the Bible belongs to him. Therefore, the seal signifies ownership. When we believed in the Lord Jesus, the Spirit of God sealed us. This signifies that God is our owner and that we belong to Him.]

B. Bearing the Image of God

[Every seal has an image. If the seal is square, then the image is also square. The Spirit as the seal of God upon us bears the image of God. This implies that the seal of the Holy Spirit is the expression of God. When you bear the Holy Spirit as the seal of God upon you, you bear the image of God and the expression of God.] Yet, if you check your daily living you must admit that you have very little expression of God. When you are quarreling with your parents do you bear the image of God?

[Many of us can testify from experience that when we believed in the Lord Jesus, we realized that we had been sealed in our spirit. However, in our mind, emotion, and will there was no sealing. At the time we believed in the Lord Jesus, the Spirit came into our spirit and sealed us there. For this reason the Bible says that we were sealed. However, not every part of our being was sealed, but just one part, our spirit. For a long time after we were saved, there continued to be no sealing in our mind, emotion, or will. But Ephesians 1 says that we were sealed unto redemption.] This is not our initial redemption but the redemption or glorification of our body. [The word "unto" means "resulting in" or "with a view to." Therefore, the sealing in our spirit is with a view to the redemption of our body. This implies that the sealing is spreading within us. It begins in our spirit and it is spreading into our mind, emotion, and will.]

[We have a living seal in us; it is constantly moving. After the Spirit seals one part of us, He desires to seal another part and then another. He wants to seal every part of our being. Until this is completed, the spreading of the sealing will continue.] [Are you under the Spirit's sealing today? Is it still going on within you? We need to have the assurance that the sealing of the Spirit is spreading in our being. When our whole being has been sealed, we shall be ready for the redemption of the body.]

III. THE PLEDGING

After the anointing, 2 Corinthians 1 mentions the sealing. Along with the anointing and sealing is the pledging. Ephesians 1:14 says that the Spirit is the pledge of our inheritance.

A. A Sample and a Foretaste

[In ancient times, the Greek word for pledge was used in the purchase of land. The seller gave the buyer a sample of the soil from the land being purchased. Hence, a pledge, according to ancient Greek usage, was also a sample. The Holy Spirit is the sample of what we shall inherit of God in full.

The Greek word for "pledge" is somewhat equal to today's down payment, which indicates good faith and is a guarantee of coming payments. Pledge, earnest, and guarantee—all these words are about the same in meaning, all referring to a payment that guarantees the balance. But the Greek word in addition signifies a sample, a foretaste. Some translators prefer the word "foretaste." By enjoying the sample we have a foretaste of what is coming. Suppose someone gives me ten peaches from his peach orchard. These peaches are a sample and a foretaste of the produce of the whole orchard. As those who are to inherit God, we have the Holy Spirit as a pledge, guarantee, earnest, and down payment of our inheritance. At the same time the Holy Spirit is also a sample and a foretaste. The foretaste gives us a taste of God; the full taste is yet to come.]

B. Given for Our Enjoyment

[The pledging of the Spirit is given for our enjoyment. Whenever I am disappointed or depressed, the pledging comes in to uplift me. I experience this pledging daily, even hourly. Pledging also means that something is given to us as a guarantee. Through the Spirit's pledging, we are encouraged and stirred up. Whenever we feel that the situation is hopeless, the pledging fills us with hope.]

[Probably in your whole Christian life you have never heard a message on the pledging of the Spirit. According to my experience, the Holy Spirit is constantly pledging within me, giving me more of God and more of Christ. The more I receive of Christ, the more my appetite for Him increases. Some may admit that they do not have a very large appetite for Christ. The reason for this is that they do not care for the pledging of the Spirit. We need to care not only for the anointing and the sealing, but also for the pledging. We need to say, "O Lord Jesus, You are so sweet. Amen, Lord." If we do this, the sense of the Spirit's pledging will increase within us. What a real experience this is!]

IV. A MUTUAL INHERITANCE

[We need both the sealing and the pledging because in God's work on us two kinds of inheritances are involved. Ephesians 1:11 indicates that we were made God's inheritance, and verse 14, that God is our inheritance. Our inheritance is God Himself. In God's economy we are an inheritance to God, and God is an inheritance to us. This is a mutual inheritance.] [The Spirit in us as a seal is God's guarantee that we shall be His inheritance (Eph. 1:13); the Spirit as a pledge in us is our guarantee that God will be our inheritance for eternity. The New Jerusalem will be a mutual dwelling place and also a mutual enjoyment in which we will enjoy God as our eternal inheritance and He will enjoy us as His eternal possession; this is the consummation of His being dispensed into us and of our being constituted with Him.]

SUMMARY

The anointing, sealing, and pledging describe three aspects of the Spirit's work in the believers. The anointing is the moving of the compound Spirit in us. It adds the divine element and essence to us. The Holy Spirit is also a living seal in us indicating that we belong to God. This sealing continues in us until we fully bear the image of God in our entire being. Furthermore, the Spirit is the pledge, the foretaste of the full taste of the enjoyment of God that we will inherit. The Spirit as a seal in us is God's guarantee that we shall be His inheritance; the Spirit as the pledge in us is our guarantee that God will be our inheritance for eternity.

Questions

1. What ground do we have for saying that the anointing refers to the moving of the compound Spirit?

2. Explain what we mean by the "paining" work of the Spirit.

3. What are the two aspects of the Spirit as a seal in us?

4. How does Ephesians 1:13-14 indicate that the sealing in us is still going on?

5. What is the Greek origin of the word "pledge"? What does this tell us about the Spirit in us?

6. Describe the two kinds of inheritances and how the Spirit is the pledge and seal to guarantee these inheritances.

Quoted Portions
from (Lee/LSM) Publications

1. *Life-study of First John,* pp. 160, 178, 283.

2. *The Spirit and the Body,* pp. 50-51.

3. *Life-study of Ephesians,* pp. 106, 108, 111, 114, 116, 118, 113.

4. *1985 Winter Training Message Abstracts,* p. 14.

THE SPIRIT'S WORK IN THE BELIEVERS (5)—
EMPOWERING AND SUPPLYING THEM
TO SPEAK CHRIST

Scripture Reading

1 Cor. 9:16; Acts 1:8; 1 Cor. 2:4; 1 Thes. 1:5; Acts 4:31

Outline

I. Christians being a speaking people
  A. Witnesses of the living Christ
  B. With the Spirit upon us and within us
II. Preaching the gospel
  A. In power, in the Holy Spirit, and in much assurance
  B. Our power—the Triune God as the Spirit
  C. With prayer, the Spirit, and boldness
  D. With a deposit of the living and rich Word
  E. The young saints preaching with power
III. Speaking Christ
  A. To all our relatives
  B. To everyone, everywhere

Text

I. CHRISTIANS BEING A SPEAKING PEOPLE

In the previous four lessons we have seen the essential work of the Spirit within the believers. But we know that there is the economical aspect of the Spirit as well. God's economical Spirit of power is mainly for speaking. He is the speaking Spirit. In 1 Corinthians 9:16 Paul said, "Necessity is laid upon me; for woe to me if I do not preach the gospel."

[We all have to realize that it is God's desire that we Christians should be a speaking people, and we have to try our best to fulfill His desire.]

A. Witnesses of the Living Christ

[In Acts 1:8, the Lord Jesus told the disciples, "But you shall receive power when the Holy Spirit has come upon you, and you shall be My witnesses both in Jerusalem, and in all Judea and Samaria, and unto the remotest part of the earth."] [Not just in our meetings, but even in our daily life, we must be people all the time speaking Christ, all the time speaking for Christ, and all the time speaking forth Christ. Whenever and wherever we open up our mouths, we speak Christ, we speak for Christ, and we speak forth Christ.... A witness is a speaking one, one who only speaks things concerning the one he is testifying. We are His witnesses and we have to speak Him, speak for Him, and speak forth Him on every occasion. Even when young ones go to their grandparents, they should not speak that much concerning other things. They should speak Christ, speak for Christ, and speak forth Christ.]

B. With the Spirit Upon Us and Within Us

[According to the principle revealed in the Scriptures, to speak God, to speak forth Christ, and to speak for Christ, surely we need the Spirit. Without the Spirit, we would not speak, and even if we would speak, we would feel shameful. When you talk about science, geography, history, or the political situation, the more you talk, the more you feel quite proud. There is no restriction or frustration in speaking about these things. But whenever you speak about Jesus, the feeling of shame follows right away. It seems hard to open up your mouth to speak about Jesus to people. Unless we have the Spirit, it is really hard for us to speak Christ. But when we are filled with the Spirit, we become crazy; we like to speak things concerning Christ to people.]

[To speak we need the Spirit. This Spirit is upon us and this Spirit is within us. Hallelujah! We were baptized in the Spirit; therefore, the Spirit is upon us. We are also drinking the Spirit; therefore, the Spirit is in us. We have the Spirit. Now we just need to exercise, to amen what the Bible says. The Bible says the Spirit is upon us. We say, "Amen." The Bible says the Spirit is within us. We say, "Amen." We do exercise such a spirit to realize that we are really in the spirit, and the Spirit is upon us and is also within us. When I speak, He is speaking in my speaking. We have to practice this all the day long. If there is no one to speak to, just speak to the angels in the air or the demons around you.]

II. PREACHING THE GOSPEL

A. In Power, in the Holy Spirit, and in Much Assurance

In 1 Corinthians 2:4 Paul said, "My speech and my preaching were not in persuasive words of wisdom, but in demonstration of the Spirit and of power." In 1 Thessalonians 1:5 he said, "Our gospel did not come to you in word only, but also in power, and in the Holy Spirit, and in much assurance, even as you know what kind of men we were among you for your sake."

[We all should learn that to preach the gospel we must preach in power, in the Holy Spirit, and in much assurance. As we preach the gospel, we need to have the assurance that it is a saving gospel. The gospel we preach is able to save others. Before sinners can believe in the gospel, we ourselves must believe it. We must believe that the gospel is able to save sinners. The expression on the faces of the opposing ones is a lie. We must have the assurance that the gospel we are preaching can save even these opposers.]

B. Our Power—the Triune God as the Spirit

[Actually, our power is the Triune God as the Spirit. Do you not believe that the Triune God is with us? I believe that He is with me in my speaking. When I am about to minister, I usually pray, "Lord, vindicate the fact that You are one spirit with me. Lord, I want to practice being one spirit with You. Lord, make it real that in my speaking You are one spirit with me. Lord, speak Your word in my speaking." This is the way I pray before giving a message. Therefore, I believe that while I am speaking, He is one spirit with me and that He is speaking in my speaking. This is the real power.]

C. With Prayer, the Spirit, and Boldness

[When we speak the word of God, we have to speak it with boldness. In Acts 4:31 boldness is used for the speaking of the word of God. This boldness is very much related to the Spirit, and the Spirit is related to prayer. This one verse is comprised of these three things. While they were beseeching, that is, while they were asking, petitioning, or praying to God, they were filled economically and outwardly with the Spirit of power. Through their prayer they experienced the Spirit. With the Spirit they spoke the word of God with boldness. You can see that the speaking of God's word here is involved in three things: prayer, the Spirit, and boldness. You could not have boldness without the Spirit, and you could not experience the Spirit without praying. Prayer brings us the Spirit, and the Spirit is the boldness. It is not only that the Spirit gives us boldness, but the Spirit Himself is the boldness. Sometimes we are timid because we are short of the Spirit. Because we are short of the Spirit, we do not have the boldness. Boldness always comes from the Spirit, and the Spirit comes from our prayer. These three things, prayer, the Spirit, and boldness, are all wrapped up with our speaking. We have to learn to pray that we may get the Spirit. Then we will have the boldness to speak the word of God.]

D. With a Deposit of the Living and Rich Word

[As Christians, we are witnesses of Christ. We should speak Him, making a habit of this. When you go to visit your aunt, forget about current events in the news and speak Christ to her. Build up such a habit. You have to believe that when you speak, the Holy Spirit always follows your speaking and honors your speaking, and people will be saved. Learn to speak the living word and learn to speak the rich word. Do not say, "Auntie, you have to believe in the Lord Jesus, otherwise you will go to hell." This kind of speaking will offend people. You have to learn to speak the rich Christ. Tell your aunt that five years ago you never knew how much the Lord Jesus is to you. Tell her by listing all the rich items of Christ.

You may tell her, "Now I know Christ is God's power and wisdom to me, and He is my righteousness, my sanctification, and my redemption."

If you are going to speak such a rich word you have to study 1 Corinthians 1. Learn to pick up the riches in the Word.] [You should not trust in some kind of inspiration. Suppose you have never learned English, yet you trust in spiritual inspiration to enable you to speak it. I assure you, you could be waiting until the Lord comes back, and you would still not be speaking English.]

If you cannot remember so much, you can simply read to her from the Recovery Version. Read some verses and read some of the rich footnotes that you have enjoyed. In fact, this is often better than your own speaking.

E. The Young Saints Preaching with Power

[Perhaps you would say, "Brother Lee, you have been in the Word for over fifty years. How can we be powerful in preaching the gospel if we are still young in the Lord?" Let me testify to you that even when I was young my speaking was powerful because of these three matters of prayer, the Word, and the Spirit, the anointing. This indicates that even the young saints can preach the gospel with power and impact if they trust in prayer, the Word, and the Spirit.

Young saints, you can take a portion of the Word and preach it to others. Only do not trust in any eloquence you might have. Those who are eloquent in speaking may not have any power or impact. But those who are not eloquent, and who may even mispronounce words, may have impact and power in their gospel preaching. If we trust in prayer, the Word, and the Spirit, the Lord may even use speaking with the wrong pronunciation of words to save others.]

III. SPEAKING CHRIST

A. To All Our Relatives

[Dear saints, now we are in the Lord's recovery and I do believe that now is the time for the Lord to carry out His up-to-date move. All of us in the Lord's recovery have to speak

Christ in our daily life to our parents, our children, our cousins, and our in-laws. We all owe so much to our relatives. Try to write a list of all the names of your relatives. Among these names maybe twenty percent are saved, and the rest are remaining in unbelief. They need your speaking. All of your relatives need the real help rendered by your speaking of Christ. Do not preach in a religious way, but speak Christ to your relatives in a living way. Speak to your father. Speak to your mother. Speak to your aunt. Speak to your uncle. Speak to your brother. Even if both you and your brother are Christians, you still need to speak one to another. Let your parents hear your speaking. Do not talk about computers, physics, or mathematics, but only Christ. He is the unique treasure! Speak about Jesus, Christ, the life-giving Spirit, the all-inclusive, processed Triune God. Your parents would marvel at such a speaking.]

B. To Everyone, Everywhere

[Continue to speak Christ every day. All human beings today need Christ, yet we need to speak to them. Speak in a living way, in a practical way, according to your experience of Him.] Speak at your school, [in your office, at the coffee break, at your lunch break, at least five minutes every day, five days a week, four weeks a month. At least twenty times monthly you could speak Christ to them.]

[We believe that today the Lord is the processed Spirit who dwells in us and also upon us. It does not matter whether this Spirit is sensed by us. We believe that while we are serving Him and speaking for Him, especially as we are speaking Him forth, He is with us. We have the Lord's presence within us as the anointing. Through prayer, the Word, and the Spirit, we can have true power and impact.] If we would be faithful to speak in this way, surely many of our dear friends and relatives would be brought to the Lord.

SUMMARY

God desires that we Christians would be a speaking people. We must be a people all the time speaking Christ; we must be witnesses of the One in whom we have believed. To speak we need to have the Spirit. The Spirit is within us and upon us, and so we simply need to exercise our spirit. We get the Spirit through prayer. Then the Spirit is our power and boldness in preaching the gospel. The content of our speaking must be the living and rich Word. Even the young saints can preach with power and impact if they would trust in prayer, the Word, and the Spirit.

Questions

1. What does it mean to be a witness?

2. What is our power and boldness in speaking? How do we receive it?

3. What are the three things that we trust in for our gospel preaching to have power and impact?

Quoted Portions
from (Lee/LSM) Publications

1. *The Up-to-Date Move of the Lord,* p. 53.

2. *The Divine Speaking,* p. 19.

3. *The Up-to-Date Move of the Lord,* pp. 52, 53, 59.

4. *Life-study of First Thessalonians,* pp. 12-13.

5. *Life-study of Acts,* p. 429.

6. *The Up-to-Date Move of the Lord,* pp. 73-74, 78, 75.

7. *Life-study of Acts,* p. 430.

8. *The Divine Speaking,* pp. 25-26.

9. *Life-study of Acts,* p. 428.

Lesson Twelve

THE SPIRIT AND THE WORD

Scripture Reading

John 6:63; 2 Tim. 3:16; Eph. 6:17-18; 5:18-19; Col. 3:16; Acts 6:7; 12:24; 19:20; 8:1, 4; 4:31

Outline

 I. Receiving the Spirit through the Word
 II. Two extremes
   A. Fundamentalists
   B. Pentecostalists
III. The Spirit embodied in the Word
   A. The spoken words being the embodiment of the life-giving Spirit
   B. The Scripture being God's breath
   C. The Spirit and the Word being one
 IV. Experiencing the fire in the Word by pray-reading
  V. Ministering the Word by the Spirit
   A. The word growing and multiplying
   B. The need to be full of the Word
   C. The Spirit within and the Word outside
 VI. The daily need to touch the Spirit in the Word

Text

I. RECEIVING THE SPIRIT THROUGH THE WORD

[We have seen that the Holy Spirit is the Triune God reaching us in a consummate way. When the Holy Spirit reaches us, the Triune God is with us. The Spirit, however, is abstract and mysterious. Hence, it is important to see that the Spirit is embodied in the Word. Now if we would live Christ, we need to experience the Spirit within and enjoy the Word without.]

[In our Christian experience, the Word and the Spirit must always be one. It is an utter falsehood to say that we take the

Spirit without taking the Word. Without taking the Word, we cannot have the Spirit. In my experience, I receive the Spirit mostly through the Word. As I contact the Word in a living way, it becomes the Spirit to me. However, some take the Bible without the Spirit. This also is wrong. Those who wish to grow flowers need both the seeds and the life contained in the seeds. It is impossible to separate the life within the seeds from the seeds themselves. In order to have the life, we must take the seeds. The relationship between the Word and the Spirit is like that between the seeds and the life. We must have both. The Lord Jesus is both the Spirit and the Word. He is not the Spirit without being the Word, nor the Word without being the Spirit.]

II. TWO EXTREMES

[Concerning the Spirit, there are two extremes, one found among fundamentalists and the other among Pentecostalists.]

A. Fundamentalists

[Because they are afraid of the experience of the Spirit, certain fundamental Christians care primarily for Bible doctrine. But to have only the doctrine of the Bible without the Spirit is to have a lifeless body. The Spirit is embodied in the Word. Hence, the Word may be called the body of the Spirit. To separate the Spirit from the Word is to have a lifeless body. The Spirit is the life content of the Bible. Apart from the Spirit, the Bible is dead letters. Nevertheless, fundamental Christians are often afraid to hear about the experience of Christ, the Spirit, and the inner life. They represent one extreme.]

B. Pentecostalists

[The Pentecostalists represent another extreme. They may neglect the Word and emphasize the Spirit in an abnormal, unbalanced way.] [Their attention is fully occupied by their thought of the Spirit. They do not see that without the Word, the Spirit is in vain. We all have to realize the Spirit comes after the Word.]

[We should not be at either extreme, but should be balanced, caring both for the Spirit and the Word. Within, we have the Spirit, and in our hands we have the Word, the Bible.]

III. THE SPIRIT EMBODIED IN THE WORD

A. The Spoken Words Being the Embodiment of the Life-giving Spirit

We can say that the Spirit and the Word are one because this is clearly revealed in the Bible. The Lord Jesus said, "The words which I have spoken unto you are spirit and are life" (John 6:63). [The Spirit is living and real, but rather mysterious, intangible, and difficult for people to apprehend, but the words are substantial. Firstly, the Lord indicated that for giving life He would become the Spirit. ["It is the Spirit who gives life." John 6:63a] Then He said that the words He speaks are spirit and life. This shows that His spoken words are the embodiment of the life-giving Spirit. He is now the life-giving Spirit in resurrection, and the Spirit is embodied in His words. When we receive His words by exercising our spirit, we receive the Spirit who is life.]

B. The Scripture Being God's Breath

[Second Timothy 3:16 says that all Scripture is God-breathed. Every word of the Bible is the breath of God. We have pointed out that this breath is the *pneuma,* the Spirit. Thus, because both the Word and the Spirit are the breath of God, they are truly one. The Spirit is the breath of God, and the Word also is God's breath. Furthermore, God's breath is His *pneuma,* the Spirit. On the one hand, the Word of God is the Spirit; on the other hand, the Spirit of God is the Word.]

C. The Word and the Spirit Being One

Furthermore, Ephesians 6:17 even identifies the Word as the Spirit. "And receive the helmet of salvation, and the sword of the Spirit which is the word of God." In this verse the Spirit and the Word are one thing.

[Ephesians 5:18-19 says that when we are filled with the

Spirit, we will sing hymns and songs. But Colossians 3:16 says that when we are filled with the *Word,* we will sing hymns and songs. Ephesians and Colossians are "sister books." They always go together. Ephesians says that when we are filled with the Spirit, we will sing. Colossians says that when we are filled with the Word, we will sing. When we compare these two parts of the Bible, we realize that the Spirit is the Word and the Word is the Spirit!]

IV. EXPERIENCING THE FIRE
IN THE WORD BY PRAY-READING

[Let us use for an illustration a match. The match stick, it is true, is made of wood, but in essence the match is really phosphorus....Now suppose I want to use the match: what shall I do? Of course, I must strike it. But how shall I strike it? If I strike it, using the end without the phosphorus, though I strike till eternity I will get no light. I am using the wrong end. The Bible is the match, and the Lord Jesus, the Spirit, is the phosphorus. The wooden stick may be likened to the black and white letters, the words in the Bible, which hold Christ as the phosphorus, the heavenly day-star. How can we make the phosphorus take fire and shine? We must use the right end of the match, and we must strike it on the right spot. The right end is the Holy Spirit, and the right spot is our human spirit.]

Ephesians 6:17-18 tells us that we should receive "the sword of the Spirit which is the word of God, by means of all prayer and petition, praying at every time in spirit." [When we read the Word, we should mingle our reading with prayer. As we exercise our eyes and our mind, we should also exercise our spirit to touch the Spirit. Then all that is in the Word will become in our experience the bountiful supply of the Spirit.]

[If we fail to exercise our spirit in reading the Word, we fail to "strike" the "match" in our spirit. As a result, the "phosphorus," the Spirit embodied in the Word, does not ignite. If we want to experience the phosphorus embodied in the match, the Spirit embodied in the Word, we need to exercise our spirit to pray-read the Word. Then we shall strike the match in the right place and experience the fire in the Word.

We can testify that by taking the Word in the proper way, exercising our spirit, we experience the burning in our spirit.]

V. MINISTERING THE WORD BY THE SPIRIT

A. The Word Growing and Multiplying

[In Acts we are told three times that the word grew and that the word multiplied (Acts 6:7; 12:24; 19:20). A lifeless thing can never grow but the word grows. Actually, the multiplication of the disciples depends upon the growth of the word. However, many who read Acts would mostly pay their attention to the Spirit. No doubt, the Spirit is stressed in Acts. But those who received the Spirit did not go out and preach the Spirit. Rather, they preached the word. Many verses in Acts tell us that what was preached and taught by the first group of believers was the word. The scattered ones in Acts 8 went out to bring the good news of the word (v. 1). People believed in the word, received the word, and the word became so prevailing in that it grew and multiplied.]

B. The Need to Be Full of the Word

[I want to impress you that the divine Word is what we really need and we should be one with the Word, full of the Word, saturated with the Word, and constituted with the Word. Then when we minister, we minister the Word by the Spirit. We do not minister the Spirit by the Word, but we minister the Word by the Spirit. In chapter four of Acts, while the disciples and the apostles were praying, they were filled with the Spirit and began to speak the word with boldness (Acts 4:31). They did not teach or preach the Spirit; the Spirit was only the power for them to preach the word.]

C. The Spirit Within and the Word Outside

In the last lesson we pointed out that in order to preach the gospel effectively we must gain a rich deposit from the Word. Now we see more clearly why this is so crucial. We surely need the Spirit's empowering, but it is the Word that we must preach.

[We have the Holy Spirit in our spirit, and we have the

Holy Word, the Bible, in our hands. These should not be two things, but two ends of one thing. The end within us is the Spirit; the end outside of us is the Word. When the Word enters our spirit it becomes the Spirit, and when the Spirit is expressed from our mouth it becomes the Word.]

VI. THE DAILY NEED TO TOUCH
THE SPIRIT IN THE WORD

Our need, then, is to spend time every day to touch the Spirit in the Word. Even if we take as little as ten minutes to pray-read a portion of the Word, we shall receive nourishment. At the very least, we should do this every morning. The morning is the best time. Before you go to school, before you do anything, pray to touch the Lord, apply His precious blood, and open the Bible to receive the Spirit through the Word.

[As saved and regenerated ones, we have the Spirit of God in our spirit. Thus, when we exercise our spirit in pray-reading the Word, we apply the Word to us and mingle the Word and the Spirit. Immediately, we receive the bountiful supply of the Spirit.]

Praise the Lord! The all-inclusive, compound, life-giving, indwelling, sevenfold intensified Spirit is embodied in the Word! Eventually you will find that ten minutes is too short a time.

SUMMARY

The Spirit is rather abstract and mysterious, but the Word of God is concrete and in our hands. The Lord Jesus is both the Spirit and the Word. Without taking the Word, we cannot have the Spirit, because the Spirit is embodied in the Word. If we would receive the Spirit through the Word, we must take the Word by exercising our spirit. Although the Spirit is our power for preaching, the Word is what we must preach. Every day we need to open the Bible to receive the Spirit through the Word.

Questions

1. Describe the two extremes concerning the Spirit among Christians. What is the proper balance?

2. What do we mean when we say that the Spirit is embodied in the Word?

3. Give three portions of Scripture that indicate that the Spirit and the Word are one. Briefly explain each portion.

4. Why is it so important that we exercise our spirit when we read the Bible?

5. How does the book of Acts show us that the Word is something living?

6. Why do we need both the Spirit and the Word for our gospel preaching?

Quoted Portions
from (Lee/LSM) Publications

1. *Life-study of Philippians,* p. 338.

2. *Life-study of Ephesians,* pp. 548-549.

3. *Life-study of Philippians,* p. 362.

4. *Fellowship Concerning the Lord's Up-to-Date Move, Elders' Training, Book 5,* pp. 41-42.

5. *Life-study of Philippians,* p. 309.

6. *Life-study of John,* p. 200.

7. *Life-study of Philippians,* p. 307.

8. *The Stream,* Vol. 5, No. 2, May 1, 1967, p. 9.

9. *Christ Versus Religion,* pp. 106-107.

10. *Life-study of Philippians,* pp. 319, 399.

11. *Fellowship Concerning the Lord's Up-to-Date Move, Elders' Training, Book 5,* pp. 38-39.

12. *Christ Versus Religion,* p. 104.

13. *Life-study of Philippians,* pp. 310-311.

Lesson Thirteen

THE HUMAN SPIRIT

Scripture Reading

Prov. 20:27; Job 32:8; Zech. 12:1; Mal. 2:15; Rom. 1:9;
Gal. 6:18; Rom. 8:16; 1 Cor. 2:11; John 4:24; Psa. 51:10;
1 Cor. 5:3; Eph. 6:18; 2 Tim. 1:7

Outline

I. The human spirit in the Scripture
II. The human spirit
    A. Being the dwelling place of the Holy Spirit
    B. Being the strategic point of the inner life
    C. Being the receiving organ
III. The three parts of the spirit—the conscience, intuition, and fellowship
IV. The importance of the conscience
    A. Maintaining a transparent conscience
    B. Dealing with the conscience by thorough confession
V. The effect of a purified conscience

Text

We have seen a great deal about the divine Spirit, the Spirit of God. But the Bible also speaks of another spirit—the human spirit, the spirit of man.

I. THE HUMAN SPIRIT IN THE SCRIPTURE

Even among Christians there is an inadequate understanding and appreciation of the human spirit. Many have never even heard that they have a human spirit! Both the Old Testament and the New Testament, however, have many verses concerning this matter.

Proverbs 20:27 says, "The spirit of man is the lamp of the Lord, searching all his innermost parts." Job 32:8 tells us "there is a spirit in man." Psalm 31:5 says, "Into thy hand I commend my spirit." We should all know Zechariah 12:1 which says that the Lord "stretches forth the heavens, and lays the foundations of the earth, and forms the spirit of man within him." We are told to "take heed to your spirit" in Malachi 2:15. There are many other verses in the Old Testament about the spirit of man.

In the New Testament Paul often spoke of "my spirit" (Rom. 1:9; 1 Cor. 14:14; 16:18; 2 Cor. 2:13), "your spirit" (Gal. 6:18; Phil. 4:23; 1 Thes. 5:23; 2 Tim. 4:22), and "our spirit" (Rom. 8:16). First Corinthians 2:11 speaks of "the spirit of man." It is clear that the spirit mentioned in all these verses does not refer to the divine Spirit but to the human spirit, *our* spirit.

II. THE HUMAN SPIRIT

A. Being the Dwelling Place of the Holy Spirit

[Why are we emphasizing the difference between the Holy Spirit and the human spirit? It is because our greatest problem is that we do not know the indwelling Spirit or realize that the human spirit is the very dwelling place of the Holy Spirit; neither do we know that these two spirits are being mingled together as one Spirit. This is a pity! It is the mark of God's economy, and many Christians are missing this mark. It is like a house that is inaccessible because the key is missing. Only the key will open the house to us that we may enjoy everything in it. For centuries the enemy has covered the key. What is the key? It is that *our human spirit is the dwelling place* of the Holy Spirit, and that our human spirit is one with the wonderful Holy Spirit.]

B. Being the Strategic Point of the Inner Life

[The human spirit is the strategic point for the inner life. We all have to know our human spirit. It is here that we have been born again and it is here that we worship God. "God is Spirit; and those who worship Him must worship in spirit" (John 4:24), not in the Holy Spirit, but in our human spirit. In our reborn human spirit we worship God, we serve God, we fellowship with one another, and we grow in life. We even have the church life here.]

C. Being the Receiving Organ

[Man can be likened to a radio. The Holy Spirit is like the heavenly radio waves. The spirit in man is like the radio receiver. The receiver is our spirit. God has done His part, and we have to take care of our spirit. We have to cooperate with God by preparing the proper organ to receive what He is, what He has done, and what He is going to do. There is no need for us to take care of the side of the Holy Spirit. That has been fully taken care of by God. We simply need to take care of our side, the human spirit.]

III. THE THREE PARTS OF THE SPIRIT—
THE CONSCIENCE, FELLOWSHIP, AND INTUITION

Let us go on to see something about the composition of the human spirit. [The spirit is a complete unit, composed of three parts or functions: conscience, fellowship, and intuition. The shaded area in the diagram below illustrates the parts of the spirit.]

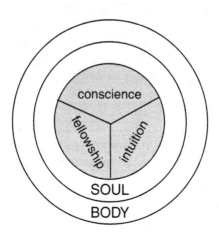

[The conscience is found in Romans 9:1, "My conscience bearing witness with me in the Holy Spirit." Comparing Romans 9:1 with Romans 8:16, the conscience is located in the human spirit. On the one hand, the Holy Spirit bears witness with our spirit. On the other hand, our conscience bears witness with the Holy Spirit. This proves that the conscience must be a function of our spirit.]

[It is easy to understand the *conscience*. We are all familiar with this. To perceive right from wrong is one function of the conscience (Psa. 51:10; 34:18). To condemn or to justify is another one of its functions (1 Cor. 5:3). It is also easy to comprehend the *fellowship*. The fellowship is our communion with God (John 4:24; Rom. 1:9). Within our spirit, such a function makes it possible to contact God (Eph. 6:18; Luke 1:47; 1 Cor. 6:17). In a simple word, fellowship is to touch God. But it is not very easy to understand the intuition. Intuition means to have a direct sense or knowledge (Mark 2:8). There is such a direct sense in our spirit, regardless of reason, circumstances, or background. It is a sense without reason, a sense that is not "reasonable" (1 Cor. 2:11). It is a direct sense of God and a direct knowledge from God. This function is what we call the intuition of the spirit. Thus, the spirit is known by the functions of the conscience, the fellowship, and the intuition.]

IV. THE IMPORTANCE OF THE CONSCIENCE

A. Maintaining a Transparent Conscience

The conscience is the leading part of our spirit. [If we are wrong in the conscience, the fellowship is broken, and when the fellowship is broken, the intuition does not function. The dealing with the conscience is therefore very basic. A transparent conscience will bring us into the presence of the Lord, resulting in a living fellowship with Him. Through this living fellowship, it is easy for our spirit to sense the will of God directly—this is the function of the intuition.]

[Of all God's creatures, only human beings have a conscience. This is the part within that either accuses or excuses you (cf. Rom. 2:15). When you deal with your conscience, you are dealing with both your spirit and your heart. If your conscience has never been dealt with, you are of no use to the Lord. A radio has a little receiver, without which it will not work. The paint may be chipped, but the radio will still work as long as the receiver is good. The same is true of our conscience; it must be kept in good working order. When we first received the gospel, the Lord required that we confess our sins. Confessing our sins clears our conscience. Without repenting and confessing your sins, you could not have been saved. The Spirit of God could not have gotten into you. Once you repent and confess, the Spirit enters into you. The more thorough the confession is, the more Spirit you have within.]

B. Dealing with the Conscience
by Thorough Confession

[We need to go to the Lord to deal with our conscience. You may feel you have only one little, unimportant thing to confess. If you will just confess that one thing, that initial confession will be a little turn to lead you onto the highway. You may then find you need a long time to complete a thorough confession.

As soon as you attempt to deal with the Lord in this way, the phone may ring. Once you take care of that phone call, it will take some effort to get back on the highway of your confession. After you confess two more things, the phone may ring again, this time probably a wrong number. This is the subtle enemy. It is best to get away by yourself, away from the phone and everyone else, or at least take the phone off the hook. If you share a room with someone else, you may need to find another place so no one can disturb you.

Once you kneel or sit before the Lord and open up to Him, you will find you have miles of confession to make. You may need hours to confess all your shortcomings, weak points, evil doings, your sinfulness, your flesh. When you start cleaning your house, you may think you can finish in fifteen minutes. But when you get into it, you will find dirt and dust all over, in all the corners. You are like your house. In every corner of your being, in every room, on every shelf, there is dirt. Your eyes have been dirtied by the many sinful things you have looked at day after day. Your ears have been sullied by listening to gossip. Your mouth needs cleansing from the gossip you have spread.]

V. THE EFFECT OF A PURIFIED CONSCIENCE

[After such a confession, you will not want to go back home. You will be afraid you may hear more gossip. It takes a great deal of effort to clean a badly smeared window. Once it is clean, you will try very hard not to let it get dirty again. This is the way to keep a clear entry for Christ to come into you. This entry, your purged conscience, will keep you from gossip.... Once your conscience is purged, you can be poor in spirit. You will no longer feel you know so much. You will be humble and hungry for the real experience of the Lord. If you are proud, your spirit is not open to the Lord and He has no way to abide in you. Purging your conscience will issue in an open spirit.]

Furthermore, [your mind will be keen and your discernment clear. No one and nothing can deceive you. This is what the Scripture calls a sound, or sober, mind (2 Tim. 1:7). Whenever you hear a message, your mind will be sharp to grasp and confirm what is being said.

A purified conscience will also affect your emotion. Before you make a thorough confession of your failures and weak points, your emotion is just lukewarm.] If your emotion were cold, you would be going to places of entertainment rather than coming to meetings. [But once you have confessed, your lukewarm emotion will catch on fire. You will declare, "Lord Jesus, I love you! I am on fire for You!"

Your will also will be changed from being stubborn to being submissive. You will enjoy obeying (cf. Phil. 2:12). Whatever it is, big or small, you will be willing to obey.

With such a purified conscience, open spirit, pure heart, sober mind, loving emotion, and submissive will, there will be a flow of the Lord within your whole being. You will surely be abiding in Him and He in you. This is the way to have the Lord added to your being all day long. The key is the thorough confession.]

SUMMARY

The Bible speaks a great deal about the human spirit because our spirit is the key to experiencing the divine Spirit.

It is the dwelling place of the Holy Spirit and the organ by which we continue to receive the Spirit. Our spirit has three parts—the conscience, fellowship, and intuition. Because the conscience is the leading part of the spirit, it must be properly maintained by confession. A purified conscience helps the other parts of our inward being to function properly and keeps the Lord flowing within us.

Questions

1. Name three verses from the Old and New Testaments that use the phrase "the spirit of man."

2. What is so important about knowing the human spirit?

3. What are the three parts of the spirit? What are the functions of each?

4. What is the result of a transparent conscience?

5. Explain what is meant by "dealing with the conscience."

Quoted Portions
from (Lee/LSM) Publications

1. *The Economy of God,* p. 36.

2. *Our Human Spirit,* pp. 20, 34-35.

3. *The Economy of God,* pp. 57-58, 78.

4. *Life Messages,* pp. 37-40.

THE DIFFERENCE BETWEEN THE SPIRIT AND THE SOUL

Scripture Reading

1 Cor. 2:14-15; 1 Thes. 5:23; Gen. 2:7; Prov. 20:27;
Heb. 4:12; 2 Cor. 7:1; Eph. 2:1, 5; Heb. 9:14;
2 Tim. 4:22; Gal. 2:20

Outline

I. The soul being different from the spirit
    A. Spirit and soul and body
    B. Joints and marrow
    C. Trichotomy and dichotomy
II. The parts of man
    A. At creation
    B. After the fall
    C. In salvation
III. The Spirit as the new person

Text

[Our spirit was created by God as the organ for us to receive Him. We must not confuse it with another organ. Suppose a medical doctor considered that the stomach, the heart, the liver, and the kidneys were all synonyms for the same organ. What kind of doctor could he be!]

[If we desire to have true spiritual growth in life, we must know that the spirit and the soul are two different things, and we must be able to discern what is the spirit and what is the soul, what is spiritual and what is soulish. If we can discern the difference between the spirit and the soul, we then can deny the soul, be delivered from the soul, and live by the spirit before God.]

I. THE SOUL BEING DIFFERENT
FROM THE SPIRIT

[If we are going to know our human spirit we must see the difference between the spirit and the soul. The most important passage showing us the difference between the spirit and the soul is 1 Corinthians 2:14-15: "But a soulish man does not receive the things of the Spirit of God, for they are foolishness to him; and he is not able to know them, because they are spiritually discerned. But he who is spiritual discerns all things, and he is discerned by no one."

Verse 14 tells us clearly that the soulish man does not receive the things of the Spirit of God. The soulish man can never know anything about God. There's no possibility for the soulish man to know God, but in the following verse it says the spirit, the human spirit, knows. With the soulish man there is no possibility to know God, but with the spiritual man there is the full possibility. So by these two verses you can see the difference between the soul and the spirit. If you are a man of the soul you can never know anything of God. If you are a man of the spirit, then you know the things of God. By this passage we can see the difference between the spirit and the soul, yet so many Christians today still insist on saying that the spirit and the soul are synonymous terms. However, 1 Corinthians 2:14-15 shows that with the soul there is no possibility to know anything of God, but with the spirit there is the full possibility.]

A. Spirit and Soul and Body

[Secondly, we have 1 Thessalonians 5:23. We must open to the Word and read it. Don't listen to any man's opinion. Don't listen to any man's word. Come back to the Word of God and read it: "And the God of peace Himself sanctify you wholly, and may your spirit and soul and body be preserved complete, without blame, at the coming of our Lord Jesus Christ." This verse clearly mentions that we have three parts—the spirit and the soul and the body. Two conjunctions connect three things. There is no ground to say that the spirit is the soul.]

[In Genesis 2:7 "the Lord God formed man of the dust of the ground, and breathed into his nostrils the breath of life; and man became a living soul." Even from this verse it is clear that man has three parts. God firstly used the dust to form a physical body for man. Then He used breath to form man's spirit. The breath of life got into man and became his spirit. The spirit of man is mentioned in Proverbs 20:27. Spirit and breath in Hebrew are the same word. This indicates that the breath breathed into man became the human spirit. When these two parts, the body and spirit, came together, they produced the third part, a living soul.]

B. Joints and Marrow

[Hebrews 4:12 says, "For the word of God is living and operative and sharper than any two-edged sword, piercing even to the dividing of soul and spirit, both of joints and marrow, and able to discern the thoughts and intents of the heart." The word divides the spirit from the soul just as the sword divides the marrow from the joints which are the bones. The marrow is not the same as the bones. The marrow is something within the bones, the joints. In the same principle the spirit is something within the soul. It is easy for people to see the bones. But it is not so easy for people to realize what the marrow is. You have to break the bones to get to the marrow. In like manner, the spirit is under the covering of the soul, but it is absolutely different from the soul.]

C. Trichotomy and Dichotomy

[It is the clear teaching of Scripture that man is tripartite (1 Thes. 5:23). Nonetheless, there are two schools of theology which have arisen on this subject. One believes, as the Bible teaches, that man is a trichotomy; that is, he is made up of spirit, soul, and body. The other school maintains that man is a dichotomy; that is, he has an outer part, the body, and an inner part, the spirit or soul. In this latter school spirit, soul, and heart are considered synonyms.] We all must give up the human teaching of dichotomy and come back to the Word of God.

Let us now go on to see the parts of man and their condition at creation, after the fall, and in salvation. This will help us to understand the position of our soul in relation to our spirit.

II. THE PARTS OF MAN

A. At Creation

[At creation, man as a soul had two organs: the outward organ of his body and the inward organ of his spirit. Man's body as the outward organ was created to contact the physical world. Man's spirit as the inward organ was purposed to contact the spiritual world. Our physical body was made with dust, but our spirit was made with the breath of life. Therefore, it is not physical, but spiritual. The human life is not in the body or the spirit, but in the soul, for the soul *is* the person. Therefore, at creation, man with his soul was a soul, a human being, who had two organs: his body and his spirit.]

B. After the Fall

[Not long after God created man, man fell. When man ate the fruit of the tree of the knowledge of good and evil, Satan entered into the body of man through the fruit of that tree (Gen. 3:6), for the fruit, we know, entered man's body.] [When Satan entered man's body, he utilized it as a base to take over the soul. Man as a human being or soul, came under the influence and control of the flesh. The soul was then damaged and became the *self*. When the body became the flesh, it damaged, influenced and even led the soul into captivity. Consequently, the soul became the self. We have pointed out in chapter two] of *The Parts of Man* [that Luke 9:25 and Matthew 16:26 prove that the soul of fallen human beings is the self.]

[Now let us see the condition of man's spirit as a result of the Fall. Although the Bible clearly shows that Satan entered into man's body, using it as a base to mingle himself with the soul, we cannot find one hint in the Scriptures that Satan has ever entered man's spirit. This is very interesting. Not one verse shows that Satan has any ground in man's spirit. It seems that God must have drawn a boundary line, telling Satan to stop and go no further. Satan may be in man's body and soul, but not in his spirit.]

[Only one verse of Scripture says that man's spirit was defiled. Second Corinthians 7:1 speaks of the filthiness of flesh and spirit. Ephesians 2:1 and Colossians 2:13 tell us that we were dead in trespasses and sins. This certainly cannot mean that we were dead in body or soul, for the fact is that our bodies are still alive and our souls are still exceedingly active! Therefore, it must mean that we were deadened in our spirit. Fallen man's spirit has been defiled and even deadened, but it has never been taken over by Satan.]

C. In Salvation

[When we received the Lord Jesus as our personal Savior, we believed in Him as the One who died for our sins and thus received forgiveness. Then we were justified and reconciled to God by His death (Rom. 5:10). To be reconciled to God means that all problems between us and God have been solved. Moreover, we who were deadened in spirit have been quickened or made alive in the spirit (Eph. 2:5). By the redeeming blood of Christ, the conscience of our spirit and of our heart has been cleansed (Heb. 9:14; 10:22). All filthiness has been purged away. But something more wonderful has happened: Christ, the Lord Spirit, has entered into our spirit as our life to make our deadened spirit alive! When He entered our spirit, we received another life, the life of God, and were regenerated (John 3:6). Christ, as the all-inclusive, life-giving Spirit (1 Cor. 15:45) is now in our spirit (2 Tim. 4:22), not in our soul.]

III. THE SPIRIT AS THE NEW PERSON

[Often we Christians are not very clear about the little revelation we have received. For example, we often say that we live by the spirit. But if the spirit is still an organ and not a man with life in it, how can we live by this organ? When we say that we live by our spirit, we need to see that this means our spirit now has become a being with life in it. Our spirit has life in it, and this life is Christ. This is why Galatians 2:20 says, "No more I, but Christ lives in me." This verse does not say, "Not my life, but the life of Christ lives in me." This verse does not refer to a life, but to a person. The "I" used to be the person, but now Christ, a new person, lives in me. I used to be the person in my soul, but now Christ is the new person in my spirit.

Now that Christ is in our spirit, we still have two organs: the body and the soul. Formerly the two organs were the body and the spirit; now the second organ is no longer the spirit, but the soul. Our soul used to be our personality, and our spirit was an organ. But now our spirit is our personality, and our soul has become an organ. This is the reason we can live and walk by our spirit. In our spirit we have not merely an organ; we have the life which is Christ Himself. Christ as the life in our spirit makes our spirit a new being with a new personality. This new being is called the inner man. This inner man needs to be strengthened, empowered. Oh, we all must see this! This is crucial! I was a Christian for more than forty years before I saw this matter. Only during the past ten years have I seen that our human spirit used to be an organ, but that now it is a man. One day the Lord pointed this out to me and said, "Look, now your personality is not in the soul, but in the spirit. The personality in your soul has been crucified, put to death." When we say our soul has been crucified and that we must deny it, we do not mean that the functions of the organ of the soul have been crucified or must be denied. The functions of the soul are still present, for today the soul is an organ. It is the being, the personality, in the soul that has been crucified and dealt with. Therefore, now there is a new being, a new personality, in our spirit. This new personality is Christ Himself. Because the divine life is in our spirit, our spirit has become the new man, the inner man. How wonderful this is! We can live and walk by this new man. If this one matter is made clear to you, you will be changed.]

SUMMARY

The spirit and the soul are two different things, the spirit being something within the soul. At creation man was a soul with two organs: his body and spirit. After the fall, man's body became the flesh, his soul became the self, and his spirit was deadened. In salvation the Lord entered our spirit and enlivened it. Our soul used to be our personality, and our spirit was an organ. But now our spirit is our personality and our soul has become an organ. This new personality in our spirit is Christ Himself as the divine life.

Questions

1. What is the most important passage showing us the difference between the spirit and the soul?

2. Explain how we can see the three parts of man in Genesis 2:7.

3. Explain the teachings of trichotomy and dichotomy. Which does the Bible teach?

4. Describe the parts of man at creation, after the fall, and in salvation.

5. Briefly explain what we mean when we say the regenerated spirit is the new person?

Quoted Portions
from (Lee/LSM) Publications

1. *The Mending Ministry of John*, p. 85.

2. *The Knowledge of Life*, p. 71.

3. *Our Human Spirit*, pp. 50-51.

4. *The Mending Ministry of John*, p. 84.

5. *Our Human Spirit*, p. 52.

6. *The Completing Ministry of Paul*, p. 67.

7. *The Parts of Man*, pp. 38-43.

8. *The Spirit and the Body*, pp. 95-96.

Lesson Fifteen

DENYING THE SOUL AND TURNING
TO THE SPIRIT

Scripture Reading

Heb. 4:12; Rom. 8:4; Matt. 10:38-39; 16:24-26; 2 Cor. 11:2;
Gal. 2:20; Acts 20:19, 31; Psa. 139:17-18a

Outline

I. Denying the soul
  A. Denying the mind, emotion, and will
  B. Practicing to deny the self
  C. The life and faculties of the soul
  D. Giving up the natural life
II. The mind, emotion, and will renewed and uplifted
  A. An uplifted understanding
  B. A spiritual emotion
  C. A strong, renewed will
  D. Faculties to express the Lord
III. A life of denying the soul and turning to the spirit
  A. Taking the Lord as life
  B. Under the control of the spirit

Text

In the foregoing lesson we saw that the spirit and the soul
are two different parts of our being. Hebrews 4:12 says that
the living word of God is sharper than any two-edged sword,
piercing even to the dividing of soul and spirit. This verse
shows not only that the spirit and soul are different, but also
that there is a need for the spirit to be divided from the soul.
We must deny our soul in order to give ground to our spirit.

I. DENYING THE SOUL

[In the teaching of the New Testament, especially in the
Gospels, it always tells us that we have to deny the soul, to
lose the soul, but it never tells us that we have to deny the

spirit. In the Epistles, we are always told that we have to walk according to spirit, live in the spirit, and do things by the spirit. In the Gospels is the denying of the soul; then is the Epistles you have walking according to the spirit (Romans 8:4). The New Testament doesn't tell us to walk and live and do things in the soul.

Matthew 10:38-39 says, "And he who does not take his cross and follow after Me is not worthy of Me. He who finds his soul (the word here in Greek is *psuche,* meaning soul) shall lose it, and he who loses his soul for My sake shall find it." Then Matthew 16:24-26 says, "Then Jesus said to His disciples, If anyone desires to come after Me, let him deny himself, and take up his cross, and follow Me. For whoever desires to save his soul shall lose it; but whoever loses his soul for My sake shall find it. For what shall a man be profited if he should gain the whole world, but forfeit his soul? Or what shall a man give in exchange for his soul?" The soul must be denied.]

[In all the four Gospels the Lord told us again and again that we have to lose the soul, to deny the soul [Mark 8:35-36; Luke 9:24-25; John 12:25], but you cannot find a word telling us that we have to lose the spirit or deny the spirit. On the contrary, the Epistles charge us to walk according to spirit, to do things in the spirit, and to pray in the spirit (Rom. 8:4; Rom. 1:9; Eph. 6:18). In the teachings of the Gospels we are told to deny the soul, to lose the soul, but in the teachings of all the Epistles we have to take care of the spirit, walk in the spirit, and we have to do things, to pray in the spirit. So there is a big, big difference between the soul and the spirit.]

A. Denying the Mind, Emotion, and Will

[The soul is comprised of three parts—the mind, the emotion, and the will (see *The Economy of God,* pp. 54-56). If you deny your mind, your emotion, and your will, there is nothing left but the spirit. The self is gone. To give up your mind, emotion, and will simply means to give up yourself. To deny yourself is to deny your own thought, your opinion, your idea, your concept, your love, your wish, your will, your decision,

and your choice. To deny all this means to deny the self.]
[After we deny the self, we have the spirit. If we deny the
emotion, mind, and will, we give the opportunity, the ground,
to the spirit.]

B. Practicing to Deny the Self

[If you denied your natural thought, the spirit within you
would rise up. Because we are so much in the soul, in the mind,
emotion, and will, our human spirit does not have the chance,
the ground, to do anything. We must practice continually to
deny our mind, our emotion, and our will. When I love a
brother so much, that may be natural love. If I give up that
love, my spirit will have a chance to express something of the
Lord. If I give up something in my soul then my spirit will
express something of the Lord. This is why the Lord tells us
that we have to deny ourselves. We have to deny our soul, to
lose our soul, because we regenerated persons have another
part, an inmost part, which is the quickened, regenerated
spirit with the Holy Spirit of God indwelling it. We have such
a wonderful part of our being, a spiritual part, a living part, a
quickened part, yet we don't know it and don't give it the
chance or the ground to do anything.

If you are not happy with a certain brother, it is simply
because you are in the self. If you deny yourself you will love
that brother very much. At other times, however, you love
certain brothers so much, simply because you are in the
emotion, in the soul. If you would deny your emotion, deny
your self, your love toward that brother would be transformed from the soul into the spirit. The lesson for us to
learn today as Christians to experience life, is to learn how
to deny the soul. The soul is the self, and the self consists of
three things—the mind, emotion, and will. To deny the soul
simply means to deny your mind, emotion, and will.]

C. The Life and Faculties of the Soul

[Some might think that if we deny the soul, we will not be
able to live. But we must realize that there is a difference
between the life of the soul and the faculties of the soul. The

life of the soul is one thing, and the faculties of the soul are another thing. An illustration might help us to see this difference. I knew a married couple in China. The brother was so spiritual and the sister, as a wife, was so submissive. Whenever you went to their home or met with them, you had the sense that the husband was the life to the wife. The wife had her own life, but she gave up her own life and took her husband as the life. She never said anything on her own. She always said something according to what her husband said. If you asked her, "Sister, do you like this piano?" She would say, "My husband likes it." Perhaps you would ask, "Do you like this meeting hall?" She would respond, "My husband says it is wonderful." With her, it was always "my husband, my husband," yet she spoke. She gave up her life and took her husband as the life, yet she still used the faculties of her soul.

We brothers always thought that sister was wonderful because she always took her husband as her life. She just lost her own life. She gave up her own life, but she still used her faculties. She still used her mind, emotion, and will, but she gave up her own life and took another life as her life.]

D. Giving Up the Natural Life

[The natural life, the life of the soul, has been crucified on the cross (Gal. 2:20). Now we have to take the Lord as our life. We must give up the natural life, the life of the soul, and take the Lord in the spirit as our life. This doesn't mean, however, that we must give up the faculties of our soul, but the life of the soul. All the faculties of our soul still remain as the organs to be used by the Lord in the spirit.]

[Do not think that all thoughts come from hell or that all intents come from the self. Some thoughts come from the heavens, and some intents are for God. But mostly we have a mixture in our thoughts and intents and need the living, operative, sharp word to pierce into us and discern our thoughts and intents, revealing which are of and for the self and which are of and for God. If we are left by ourselves, we cannot discern these matters. But once we experience the living word of God, it is easy to discern the thoughts that are not of God and the intents that are of Satan.]

II. THE MIND, EMOTION, AND WILL RENEWED AND UPLIFTED

A. An Uplifted Understanding

[The more you are one with the Lord in the spirit, the more you are spiritual, the more keen you will be in your mind. Before you take the Lord as life, you are quite dull in your thinking, but if you deny yourself and take the Lord as your life, you will be very keen in your thinking. In China quite a number of older sisters never had any kind of education, yet they loved the Lord to the uttermost and knew how to give up themselves, taking the Lord as life. After two or three years they became very keen in their mind, in their understanding, especially in the things of the Lord. They became experts. But with those who have little love for the Lord, even if they have a Ph.D., there is little comprehension of spiritual things. When you talk with them about the things of the Lord, they say, "What is this? I cannot figure it out."]

B. A Spiritual Emotion

[It is the same thing with the emotion. Don't think that the Lord demands that you give up the organ, the faculty, of your emotion. The Lord demands that you give up the life of the emotion, but you have to exercise the emotion more and more. If you do love the Lord and are really filled with the Lord's Spirit, you will be very emotional. A man who is not emotional can never be spiritual. A spiritual person is a very emotional person. If you never know how to love, if you never know how to weep, if you never know how to be happy, and if you never know how to be sorry, I am afraid that you are not a Christian.

The most spiritual person is the most emotional, yet his emotion is under the control of the spirit. The apostle Paul was very emotional. He tells us that at times he wept with tears (Phil. 3:18; Acts 20:19,31). He was quite tender in feeling, in love, in mercy, and in compassion. He was tender, but he was not naturally emotional. His emotion was a spiritual emotion under the control of the spirit.]

C. A Strong, Renewed Will

[A spiritual person, on the one hand, is so keen in the mind and emotion, and on the other hand, so strong in the will. Not one spiritual person is like a jelly-fish, without any backbone. Naturally emotional people are like jelly-fish. All the spiritually emotional persons are so tender in their emotions and strong in the will. The more you are in the spirit, the stronger you will be in the will.]

D. Faculties to Express the Lord

[A spiritual person is one who is so keen in the understanding of the mind, so emotional in his love and affection, and so strong in his will. The faculties of the soul are organs used by the Spirit to express the Lord. The Lord is so wise and full of thought (Psa. 139:17-18a). A spiritual person isn't a thoughtless person. The more spiritual you are, the more thoughtful you are in the spirit. I can testify that the more I am in the spirit, the richer I am in thought. But whenever I am so much in my self, I am poor in thought.

We must realize, therefore, that it is not the mind, emotion, and will that have to be destroyed. It is the life of the soul that we must give up. This natural life, the soul life, has been put to death on the cross already (Gal. 2:20; Rom. 6:6). Now you have to take Christ, your husband (2 Cor. 11:2), as your life. You must take the divine life as your life, but the faculties of the soul still remain as organs to be used by your spirit to express the Lord Himself.]

III. A LIFE OF DENYING THE SOUL AND TURNING TO THE SPIRIT

A. Taking the Lord as Life

[As Christians we have to reject our mind, emotion, and will. We must reject ourselves and take the Lord Jesus as our life. This is done by returning to our spirit and sensing what is there in our spirit. Suppose a brother comes to talk with you. While you are listening, you must reject yourself. You must reject your natural thinking, your emotion, and your will. You have to take the Lord Jesus as your life in this particular matter by returning to your spirit, your innermost part, to sense what is there. This is the right way for us to act as a Christian, but most of us do not act in this way. Whenever a brother comes to talk with us, we exercise our mind independent of the spirit. We sometimes forget about the Lord Jesus and forget that we have a spirit. The way for a normal Christian to act, though, is to always deny the natural mind, will, and emotion, and take the Lord Jesus as his life. In everything we should return to the innermost part of our being to sense what is there.]

B. Under the Control of the Spirit

[We must learn the lesson to deny the natural mind, emotion, and will, and to put them under the control of the spirit. We deny the life of the soul and take the Lord as our life in the spirit to control and direct all the parts of the soul in order that they might be used to express the Lord Himself.]

[To deny the soul means that we turn from ourselves to the spirit. Then in the spirit we will meet Christ. Why do the four Gospels tell us negatively to deny the soul, while later all the Epistles tell us positively to live and do things in the spirit? Because today the Lord Jesus is in the spirit, and His grace is in the spirit. To follow Christ is a matter of dealing with the spirit, and this is the mark of God's economy! Oh, we need to stress again this mark of God's economy! We all must be clear that God's eternal plan is to dispense Himself into our spirit. He has done this already, for He is now in our spirit to be our life and everything. All our needs are met in this wonderful Spirit who is in our spirit.]

SUMMARY

The New Testament teaches us that we have to deny our soul. The soul is the self. To deny our soul simply means to deny our mind, our emotion, and our will and to turn to our spirit. The life of the soul is different from the faculties of the soul. We deny the life of the soul, but the faculties remain as organs to be used by the spirit to express the Lord.

Questions

1. What are the parts of the soul?

2. Explain why it is wrong to think that if we deny the soul, we also deny the faculties of the soul?

3. What is the difference between the life of the soul and the faculties of the soul?

4. What is the way that we can deny the soul life?

5. What is the result of denying our soul?

Quoted Portions
from (Lee/LSM) Publications

1. *Our Human Spirit,* pp. 53-54, 56-59.

2. *Life-study of Hebrews,* p. 272.

3. *Our Human Spirit,* pp. 59-61, 63, 62.

4. *The Economy of God,* pp. 100-101.

KNOWING OUR SPIRIT

Scripture Reading

Dan. 7:15; Rom. 8:6

Outline

I. The sense of the spirit
II. Setting the mind on the spirit—the key to death or life
    A. The sense of life
    B. The sense of peace
    C. The sense of death
III. Living in the spirit
    A. Taking care of the inner sense
    B. The Christian life according to the spirit

Text

[To speak of the body is very easy, because we can see it and touch it. To speak of the soul is also not difficult, because, though the soul is abstract, we can feel it and know it by its functions and actions, such as thinking, considering, determining, decision-making, and being pleased, angry, sorrowful, and joyful. Only when we speak of the spirit is it truly difficult. Even understanding the spirit is not easy, not to mention speaking about the spirit.]

Where is our spirit located? This we are not sure of. Daniel 7:15 tells us that our spirit is in the midst of our body but does not tell us the exact location. Nevertheless, from our experience, we know that we have a spirit in us. If we want to know the spirit directly, it is somewhat difficult, but it is comparatively easy to know the spirit itself by the senses of the spirit.

I. THE SENSE OF THE SPIRIT

[To know the spirit is to know it by the sense of the spirit.

Even up until this day, no one has ever seen electricity itself. The light of a lamp is not the electricity, but an expression, a sign of electricity. We can know electricity by its signs and expressions. Also, no one has ever seen the physical life of a person's being, but we can know the physical life by its expression and by certain senses. In the same principle, the spirit is very mysterious. You can't see it, but you can sense it. You can't see electricity, but when you touch it, you can sense it. In like manner, you can know the spirit by sensing the spirit. To sense the spirit is the way to know the spirit.]

II. SETTING THE MIND ON THE SPIRIT— THE KEY TO DEATH OR LIFE

[Romans 8 speaks of the spirit. It is difficult to find another place in the Bible which speaks of our condition in the spirit as clearly as this one. Therefore, if we want to know the spirit, it is imperative that we pay attention to this passage.]

Romans 8:6 says, "For the mind set on the flesh is death, but the mind set on the spirit is life and peace." [To set our mind—that is, to set our self—upon the flesh is death. To set our mind, or our self, upon the spirit is life and peace. Here is the key to death or life. The mind is quite neutral: it is on the fence. It may turn toward the flesh, or it may turn toward the spirit. Again, the story of the garden of Eden must be repeated. The free will can make either of two choices. To choose the tree of knowledge means death, but to choose the tree of life means life. We are between these two; we are neutral to life and death. The issue depends on our choice, our attitude. Personified Sin, representing Satan, is in the flesh; the Triune God is in the spirit after we are saved; and the self is in the mind. The secret of life or death is dependent upon our cooperating with the spirit or with the flesh. When we cooperate with the flesh, we have death; when we cooperate with the spirit, we are partakers of God, who is life.]

A. The Sense of Life

[Originally our spirit was merely the spirit of man, and it

was dead. Now, when the Spirit of God enters, He not only quickens our spirit, but also adds the life of God into our spirit. Now not only is our spirit alive, but it also has the life of God; and it is not only a spirit; it is the spirit of life. All the consciousness of life in this spirit enables us to know this spirit. When we walk by setting our mind on this spirit, and when our actions and deeds are according to this spirit, the life in this spirit will cause us to have the consciousness of this life. Since this life is of God, fresh and lively, strong with power, bright and holy, real and not empty, the sense of this life surely will make us sense the presence of God; thus we will feel fresh and lively, strong with power, bright and holy, real and not empty. When we have such feelings, we know we are minding the spirit, walking according to the spirit, and living in the spirit. Such feelings are the sense of life in our spirit, or the consciousness of our spirit of life, leading us from within to walk according to the spirit and live by the spirit. When we touch such feelings, we touch the spirit. When we heed such feelings, we heed the spirit. The spirit itself is relatively difficult for us to sense, but we can easily sense such feelings of life in the spirit. If we follow such feelings closely, we can then know the spirit and live in the spirit.

The life of God in our spirit can be said to be God Himself; therefore, the sense of this life surely will make us sense God Himself. If we live in the spirit and walk by minding the spirit, the sense of this life will cause us to feel that we are in touch with God, and that God is in us as our life, our power, and our all; thus we will be happy, restful, comfortable, and satisfied. When we thus touch God in the inner sense of life, we touch life; thereby we know we are living in the spirit and setting our mind upon the spirit.]

B. The Sense of Peace

[To set the mind on the spirit is not only life but peace. The peace mentioned in Romans 8:6 is not the peace in our outward circumstances, but the peace within us.]

[This sense of peace and the sense of life go hand in hand. The sense of life is fresh and lively; the sense of peace is

natural and at ease. The sense of life is satisfaction and fullness of vigor; the sense of peace is rest and comfort. If we
mind the spirit and walk and live by the spirit, we will not
only have the sense of life, feeling fresh, lively, satisfied and
vigorous, but also have the sense of peace, feeling natural,
restful, comfortable, and at ease. Such a sense is also the
sense of the spirit. Once we have such a sense, we may know
that we are living in the spirit. When we follow such a sense,
we follow the sense of the spirit, which means that we follow
the spirit. Such a sense enables us to know the spirit and
recognize the spirit. The more we walk according to the spirit
and live in the spirit, the richer and deeper this kind of sense
within us becomes.]

C. The Sense of Death

[There is a contrast in Romans 8:6. The apostle says that
the result of minding the flesh is death, whereas the result
of minding the spirit is life and peace. This word reveals that
just as the flesh is versus the spirit, so also the result of
minding the flesh, which is death, is opposite to the results
of minding the spirit, which are life and peace. Thus, the
apostle tells us here that death is not only the opposite of
life, but also the opposite of peace. Therefore, the sense
of death is not only the opposite of the sense of life, but also
the opposite of the sense of peace. The sense of life makes us
feel fresh, lively, satisfied and vigorous; the sense of death
makes us feel the opposite of these—old, depressed, empty
and powerless. The sense of peace makes us feel natural,
restful, comfortable, and at ease. The consciousness of
death makes us feel just the opposite of these—unnatural,
unrestful, uncomfortable, and uneasy. Thus, whenever we
feel inwardly desolate, depressed, empty, dry, weak and powerless, dark and dull, or uneasy, insecure, uncomfortable, out
of harmony, full of conflict, unnatural, sad, and bound, we
should know we are not living in the spirit; rather we are
living in the opposite of the spirit, which is the flesh. Thus,
by knowing the opposite of the spirit, we may know the
spirit itself.]

III. LIVING IN THE SPIRIT

A. Taking Care of the Inner Sense

[Don't argue with the inner sense of life and peace. Don't say that something is good, scriptural, or holy. Don't reason and don't argue that what you are doing is for the gospel or for the church. The test is—do you have the inner sense of life and peace? The more you reason with this sense, the more you argue, the more you will sense death within you. We can know the spirit just by this inner sense. If we are going to differentiate the spirit and the soul, we must deny the rational mind, emotion, and will all the time and take care of the inner sense.]

B. The Christian Life According to the Spirit

[Suppose we find something that we would like to purchase. The more we consider it, the more we feel that we would like to have it. Eventually, we make the decision to buy it. The emotion is exercised, since we like it; the mind is exercised, because we have considered it; and the will is exercised because we have made the decision to buy it. Therefore the whole soul is exercised. But when we go to buy it, something *very deep within* us protests. Our emotion likes it, our mind considers it, and our will chooses it, but something deeper within us protests. This is the spirit.]

[Whatever we do, regardless of whether we think it is right or wrong, spiritual or unspiritual, if deep within us we feel restless, insecure, empty, and depressed, it proves that we are walking by the flesh and not living in the spirit. Even in prayer and preaching, not to mention other things or doing things which are not good, if we feel empty and depressed within, dissatisfied or unhappy, then it is proof that we are praying or preaching by the flesh, not in the spirit.]

[The Christian walk, the Christian life, the Christian activity is not according to the standard of good or bad, but absolutely according to the spirit. If we would know this one thing and be ruled and controlled by it, the Lord would transform our inward being and our daily life.]

SUMMARY

The human spirit can be known by the senses of the spirit. Because God Himself is in our spirit, we sense life and peace when our mind is set on the spirit and we are living in our spirit. And when we are not in our spirit, we experience the opposite—the sense of death. The Christian life is not a matter of right and wrong; it is a matter of living by the inner sense of the spirit.

Questions

1. What are the three senses of the spirit? What verse backs this up?

2. How is the situation with our mind, flesh, and spirit like the situation in the garden of Eden?

3. Briefly describe the three senses of our spirit.

4. How should the sense of the spirit affect the way we live?

Quoted Portions
from (Lee/LSM) Publications

1. *The Knowledge of Life,* p. 59.

2. *Our Human Spirit,* pp. 65, 59.

3. *The Economy of God,* p. 148.

4. *The Knowledge of Life,* pp. 65-66.

5. *Our Human Spirit,* p. 67.

6. *The Knowledge of Life,* pp. 67-69.

7. *Our Human Spirit,* p. 69.

8. *The Stream,* Vol. 4, No. 1, February 1, 1966, p. 5.

9. *The Knowledge of Life,* p. 69.

10. *Our Human Spirit,* pp. 68-69.

Lesson Seventeen

THE MINGLED SPIRIT

Scripture Reading

1 Cor. 6:17; Rom. 8:4; 2 Tim. 4:22; 2 Cor. 3:17; Rom. 8:16

Outline

I. One spirit with the Lord
    A. Two spirits mingled as one
    B. No third nature produced
II. The Spirit witnessing with our spirit
III. Walking according to the mingled spirit

Text

[Physically we were born of our parents, but when we were regenerated, we were "born of the Spirit" (John 3:6). By believing in the Lord Jesus, our spirit was born of the Spirit. The all-inclusive Spirit came into our spirit to regenerate it with the divine life.]

I. ONE SPIRIT WITH THE LORD

[One of the greatest verses in the Bible, 1 Corinthians 6:17, says, "He that is joined to the Lord is one spirit." The implications of this verse are marvelous and far-reaching. We, the believers, are one spirit with the Lord. How tremendous! This implies that we are in Him and that He is in us. It also implies that we and He have been mingled, blended organically, to become one in life. To be one spirit with the Lord implies that we and He are a living entity. We simply do not have words to explain the significance of this verse. To say that we are one spirit with the Lord definitely does not mean that we are deified. However, it certainly does imply the mingling of divinity with humanity. In the words of #501 in *Hymns,* "God mingled with humanity lives in me my all to be." To be one spirit with the Lord means that we are blended with Him organically and mingled with Him in life.]

[The word translated spirit in Romans 8:4, and in several other verses in Romans 8, presents a problem to translators. It is hard to decide whether to regard spirit as referring to the Holy Spirit and capitalize it, or to consider that it is the human spirit and not capitalize it. The spirit here refers to the mingled spirit, our spirit mingled with the Holy Spirit. We need another size letter to denote this, neither a capital letter nor a small one! These two spirits, the divine and the human, have become one (1 Cor. 6:17; 2 Tim. 4:22; 2 Cor. 3:17).]

A. Two Spirits Mingled as One

[The Lord today is the life-giving Spirit, and we have a human spirit purposely created by God that we may take Christ as the life-giving Spirit into us. Now these two spirits have become one. This is wonderful! Our spirit is one with the Lord, because as the life-giving Spirit He indwells our spirit. But the Lord in our spirit is not like a drop of oil in water, never mingling with the water. He mingles with us in our spirit as tea mingles with water. This is why many times it is difficult to distinguish whether it is we or the Lord doing things. We have some burden, yet it seems the Lord wants to do it. It is because we are one with the Lord in our spirit. After tea is put into water, it is difficult to separate the tea from the water. That is why I call it tea-water. It is both tea and water. The two mingle as one. In the same way, the Lord Jesus as the life-giving Spirit mingles with our spirit as one. He is in us, and we are in Him. It seems that a brother is speaking, but while he is speaking, the Lord is also speaking. He speaks within that brother. His speaking is the brother's speaking, and the brother's speaking is His speaking. Eventually, a mingled one is speaking. Praise the Lord! We are really one spirit with the Lord.]

B. No Third Nature Produced

[Some Bible students and even some Bible teachers have failed to understand the matter of mingling. In ancient times there was a debate regarding the mingling of the divine

essence and the human essence in the Person of the Lord
Jesus. Some who misunderstood this mingling said that it
caused a third nature to be produced, something which is
neither divine nor human. To say that with respect to the
Lord Jesus the mingling of the divine essence and the human
essence produced a third nature, a nature that is neither fully
human nor divine, is heretical. However, we wish to make it
clear that this is not our understanding of the word "mingle."
We agree with the first definition of this word given in
Webster's unabridged dictionary; mingle—"to combine or join
(one thing with another, or two or more things together),
especially so that the original elements are distinguishable in
the combination." According to this definition, when two or
more things are mingled together, their original natures are
not lost but remain distinguishable.]

II. THE SPIRIT WITNESSING WITH OUR SPIRIT

["The Spirit Himself witnesses with our spirit that we are
the children of God" (Rom. 8:16). Now that the Spirit is within
our spirit through regeneration, He witnesses with our spirit,
testifying that we are the children of God. These two spirits
within us correspond to each other, together confirming that
we are God's children.]

[This verse does not say that the Spirit witnesses and our
spirit witnesses also. It says the Spirit witnesses with our spirit.
To say that the Spirit witnesses with our spirit is deeper than
saying that the Spirit and our spirit witness, for it indicates
that the two spirits are one. To say that the Spirit and our
spirit witness means that these spirits remain two. But to say
that the Spirit witnesses with our spirit indicates that the
two spirits have been mingled and have become one.]

[Regardless of how young or new you may be, if you are a
child of God, the Spirit of God witnesses with your spirit.
Notice that it does not say "in our spirit." If it said "in our
spirit," it would mean that only the Spirit of God witnesses,
but that our spirit does not witness. However, it says that the
Spirit witnesses with our spirit, meaning that both witness
together. The Spirit of God witnesses, and simultaneously our
spirit witnesses together with Him. This is wonderful.

Some may say, "I don't feel that the Spirit of God witnesses. Where is the Spirit of God? I don't feel Him. I don't
have any sensation that the Spirit of God is within me. I never
saw Him and I cannot feel Him. I simply cannot sense Him."
However, do you not feel that your spirit witnesses? You must
realize that as long as your spirit is witnessing it means that
the Holy Spirit also is witnessing. You cannot deny that your
spirit witnesses within you. The apostle Paul was very wise.
He said that the Spirit witnesses with our spirit. When our
spirit witnesses, that is also the witnessing of the Spirit,
because the two spirits have been mingled together as one. It
is very difficult for anyone to distinguish these two spirits.]

III. WALKING ACCORDING TO
THE MINGLED SPIRIT

[Even a young student has to learn how to experience
Christ in the study of his lesson books. He may pray, "Lord,
here is the lesson book, and tomorrow will be the final.
Lord, prove that You are one spirit with me. Lord, read this
book with me." If he does this, I assure you he will experience
Christ as his understanding and as his wisdom to take in all
the secrets of his lesson book. He will even experience Christ
as his good memory. Then the next day when he takes the
exam he does not need to be so pressed and so trembling. He
just needs to pray, "Lord, I am one with You, and even one
spirit with You. Not only in speaking, Lord, even today in the
classroom, taking the exam, I am one with You, Lord. Lord,
make it so real. Make it so real to the angels. Make it so real
to the entire universe that I am one with You." I assure you
that he will experience Christ as his wisdom and quite often
as his answer. This is the way.]

[Day by day we should cleave to the mingled spirit and do
everything according to this spirit. Whenever we walk according to the flesh we are sinners, no matter whether we regard
ourselves as good or bad. But we need not walk according to
the flesh, for we have the option of walking according to the
spirit. When we do this, we enjoy all the riches of Christ.

We daily need to practice having our being according to
the spirit. We need to apply this in our talking, in our thinking,

and in everything we do. For example, suppose a young one is wondering whether he can participate in a certain kind of athletic activity. My advice to him would be that if he can participate in that athletic activity according to the spirit, then he should go ahead and do so. As Christians, we should not decide matters according to right or wrong; rather, we should decide them according to the spirit.

The Spirit who is mingled with our spirit and according to whom we may have our very being is the wonderful Spirit of the Triune God. Such a Spirit, the realization and application of the Triune God, is now mingled with our spirit.] It [is no longer a matter of simply the divine Spirit nor of just the human spirit, but it is a matter of the divine Spirit mingled with the human spirit. Hallelujah for this marvelous mingling!]

SUMMARY

We the believers are one spirit with the Lord. We are in Him and He is in us. The Lord Jesus as the life-giving Spirit is mingled, blended organically with our spirit. In the mingling of divinity with humanity, the original natures are not lost and no third nature is produced. The Spirit witnesses with our spirit testifying that we are the children of God. Every day we should walk according to the mingled spirit.

Questions

1. What is one of the greatest verses in the Bible showing we are one spirit with the Lord?

2. Why does the word translated "spirit" in Romans 8:4 present a problem to translators of the Bible?

3. What do we mean when we say the life-giving Spirit "mingles" with our spirit?

4. Does the mingling produce a third nature?

5. Why does the Bible say the Spirit of God witnesses "with our spirit," and not "in our spirit"? What does this show us?

6. Why can we not tell if it is the Holy Spirit witnessing or if it is our spirit witnessing that we are the children of God?

Quoted Portions
from (Lee/LSM) Publications

1. *The Completing Ministry of Paul,* p. 54.

2. *Life-study of Colossians,* pp. 457-458.

3. *Life Messages,* p. 432.

4. *The Stream,* Vol. 14, No. 1, February 1, 1976, p. 10.

5. *Life-study of Luke,* pp. 5-6.

6. *The Completing Ministry of Paul,* p. 54.

7. *Life-study of Romans,* pp. 715, 218-219.

8. *The Up-to-Date Move of the Lord,* pp. 31-32.

9. *Life-study of Romans,* p. 593.

BEING FILLED IN SPIRIT

Scripture Reading

Eph. 5:18; 3:19; Acts 2:2-4; 13:52; John 14:17;
Rom. 8:11; Acts 1:8; 2:17; Eph. 5:19

Outline

I. Two aspects of the filling
II. Being willing to be used by God
III. The way to be filled
   A. By thorough confession
   B. By speaking
IV. Being filled to speak and dispense

Text

Ephesians 5:18 says, "And do not be drunk with wine, in which is dissipation, but be filled in spirit." [To be filled in spirit (v. 18) is to be filled in our regenerated spirit, the human spirit indwelt by the Spirit of God. Our spirit should not be empty, but should be filled with the riches of Christ unto all the fullness of God (3:19).... Our spirit may be empty and flat, like a flat tire. If our spirit is flat, it needs to be filled with *pneuma*. We need to go to the heavenly "filling station" and get our spirit filled with *pneuma*. In this way we shall be filled in spirit. According to chapter three, we are to be filled with the riches of Christ unto all the fullness of God. If our spirit if filled with the riches of Christ, we shall have no problems in our Christian life.]

I. TWO ASPECTS OF THE FILLING

We have seen that there are two aspects of the all-inclusive Spirit (Lesson 7). One is essential (inward) and the other is economical (outward). These two aspects of the Spirit can be seen in the matter of being filled with the Holy Spirit.

[Acts 2:2 says that the wind filled the house where the one hundred twenty were sitting. The Greek word for "filled" here is *pleroo*, a word that means to fill inwardly, as the wind filled the house.

Verses 3 and 4 say, "And there appeared to them tongues as of fire, which were divided and sat on each one of them; and they were all filled with the Holy Spirit, and they began to speak in different tongues, even as the Spirit gave them to speak out." The Greek word for "filled" in verse 4 is *pletho* (also used in 4:8, 31; 9:17; 13:9 and Luke 1:15, 41, 67). This Greek word means to fill outwardly. According to its usage in Acts, *pleroo* denotes to fill a vessel within, as the wind filled the house inwardly in verse 2; and *pletho* denotes to fill the persons outwardly, as the Spirit filled the disciples outwardly in this verse. The disciples were filled (*pleroo*) inwardly and essentially with the Spirit (13:52) for their Christian living, and they were filled (*pletho*) outwardly and economically with the Spirit for their Christian ministry. The inward filling Spirit, the essential Spirit, is in the disciples (John 14:17; Rom. 8:11), whereas the outward filling Spirit, the economical Spirit, is upon them (Acts 1:8; 2:17).] Every proper Christian should experience both kinds of filling.

[After Pentecost, the experience of the Holy Spirit inwardly as well as outwardly was fully accomplished in the Head (the Lord Jesus) as well as in the Body (represented by the apostles). From this time onward, all those who desire to experience the work of the Holy Spirit can experience both the indwelling and the outward descending of the Holy Spirit at the same time.]

II. BEING WILLING TO BE USED BY GOD

We should, however, say a word regarding the outward filling. [Actually, if from the beginning all those who are saved would be willing to abandon everything for the Lord to be used by Him, then upon being saved each one would be in a position to receive both aspects of the filling of the Holy Spirit simultaneously, as occurred in the house of Cornelius. We regret to say that today there are too few who are willing to be used by God upon being saved. Most people are satisfied with just possessing eternal life and not having to perish. They completely disregard God's work and God's plan; neither do they desire to have power to work for God and fulfill His plan.

Since man is so unwilling to be used by God, few obtain the outward filling of the Holy Spirit, causing this experience to become mysterious and rare. In fact, the outward aspect of the Holy Spirit is by no means more precious or more difficult to obtain than the Holy Spirit within, the only requirement being that we be willing to be used by God.]

III. THE WAY TO BE FILLED

A. By Thorough Confession

[In order to receive the regeneration of the Holy Spirit, we must first confess, repent, and accept the fact that Christ has died for us. Likewise, in order to receive the infilling of the Holy Spirit, we must first accept the fact that we have died with Christ. Then we must deal with sin, the world, the flesh, our self-opinion, and our natural ability, to the end that we may completely empty ourselves of these, allowing none of them to have any more place in us, but rather allowing the Holy Spirit to gain all the ground in us. If we will respond to the demand of the Holy Spirit, removing that which must be removed and forsaking that which must be forsaken, thus emptying ourselves and letting the Holy Spirit have all the ground and authority in us, then automatically the Holy Spirit will fill us, and we will subjectively experience and enjoy the infilling of the Holy Spirit.]

We all must make a thorough confession. We must come to the Lord, not occupied by so many things or persons. We should come simply to contact Him and be filled with Him. As we do, the first thing that will come up will be our sin. We will have a deep sensation that we are not right in a certain matter. As you confess, another matter may come up. Upon confessing again, a third will arise, then a fourth, and so on. Without such a time you probably could not realize how many sins you have.

We must get fully cleared up through prayer by confessing all our failures, wrongdoings, mistakes, sinful things, offenses, etc. If we have not gone to the Lord in this way for some time we may need one or even two hours to be fully cleansed. We may even need to make right any offenses with others or debts that we have accumulated. We all need to have this kind of experience.

After such a thorough confession we will be filled with the Spirit. We do not need to speak in "tongues." Neither should we wonder what will happen or how we will feel when we are filled inwardly and outwardly with the Spirit. We should just go to the Lord again and again. Every day you need this kind of clearing up. Pray, "Lord, cleanse me. Clear me up. I would like to pour out my dirt, my junk and give you all the space in me." If you would do this each day, the infilling and outpouring of the Spirit will be so fresh in your experience.

B. By Speaking

After Ephesians 5:18 says, "Be filled in spirit," verse 19 continues, "Speaking to one another in psalms and hymns and spiritual songs." [Right after "be filled in spirit" you have the word "speaking." This kind of phrase could be considered as a modifier. "Speaking to one another" modifies "be filled." How could you be filled? It is by speaking. By speaking, you will be filled in your spirit. But is it by speaking to one another in murmuring? Gossip? World news? America today? School? Family? Computers? Master's degree? Doctor's degree? Speaking in what? Speaking in psalms, long pieces like Psalm 119 which has 176 verses of 22 sections according to the Hebrew alphabet.]

[Psalms, hymns, and spiritual songs are not only for singing and psalming, but also for speaking to one another. Such speaking, singing, and psalming are not only the outflow of being filled in spirit, but also the way to be filled in spirit. Psalms are long poems, hymns are shorter ones, and spiritual songs are the shortest. All are needed in order for us to be filled with the Lord and to overflow with Him in our Christian life.

According to the New Testament, psalms, hymns, and spiritual songs are good not only for singing, but also for speaking. Sometimes we are inspired by singing. But on other occasions, speaking that is filled with *pneuma* may be more inspiring than singing. If we are flat, short of *pneuma,* then our speaking will afford no inspiration. But if we are full of *pneuma,* then our speaking will have impact and will inspire others. This is not eloquence; it is utterance with impact.]

IV. BEING FILLED TO SPEAK AND DISPENSE

[This filling is not only for your nourishment, it is for you to dispense. It is for you to generate. Every human being is made by God to propagate, to generate. Therefore, everybody has to bring forth children! Now we all have to learn how to generate, how to dispense, how to impart into others what we have received into our being. This is to reproduce, this is to generate, this is to bring forth new Christians by speaking. Therefore, speaking is generating, speaking is imparting, speaking is dispensing.]

When you speak you are filled, and when you are filled you speak! This is wonderful. When the Spirit is so fresh in our experience, people will sense something different about us. As you speak to them, they will realize something within you is so new, so different, yet so convincing. If we are cleansed by confessing, we will surely have impact and the working of the Spirit in our speaking. Be filled in spirit!

SUMMARY

The Lord charges us to be filled in spirit. This filling is of two aspects—one is inward and the other is outward. The inward filling is the essential aspect of the Spirit, whereas the outward filling is the economical aspect of the Spirit. Both are necessary for our Christian life and ministry. The way to be filled is 1) by confessing all our sins, failures, worldliness, pride, etc., and 2) by speaking. This will make us people who dispense Christ and bring forth new Christians.

Questions

1. What are the two aspects of the filling of the Holy Spirit?

2. Explain how the Greek language indicates the two aspects of the filling.

3. What is one condition that must be met in order to have the outward filling of the Spirit?

4. What is the way to be filled in spirit?

5. What should be the result of being filled?

Quoted Portions
from (Lee/LSM) Publications

1. *Life-study of Ephesians,* p. 431.

2. *Life-study of Acts,* pp. 56-57.

3. *The Experience of Life,* p. 308, 311-312, 309-310.

4. *The Up-to-Date Move of the Lord,* pp. 18-19.

5. *Life-study of Ephesians,* pp. 434-435.

6. *The Divine Speaking,* p. 52.

Lesson Nineteen

EXERCISING OUR SPIRIT

Scripture Reading

1 Tim. 4:7; 2 Tim. 1:7; 4:22; 1 Tim. 1:5; Heb. 10:22;
1 John 1:7; Eph. 6:18; 1 Thes. 5:17

Outline

I. Exercise unto godliness
  A. The exercise of the spirit
  B. More profitable than bodily exercise
II. Taking care of our conscience
  A. A good conscience
  B. The need of the cleansing blood
III. Exercising by praying
  A. Praying without ceasing by calling
  B. Pray-reading the Word
IV. Exercising our spirit in the meetings

Text

I. EXERCISE UNTO GODLINESS

A. The Exercise of the Spirit

[First Timothy 4:7 says to "exercise yourself unto godliness." Second Timothy 1:7 tells us, "God has not given us a spirit of cowardice, but of power and of love and of a sober mind." Then 2 Timothy 4:22 says, "The Lord be with your spirit." When we put all these verses together, we can see that the exercise unto godliness depends on the exercise of the spirit, where the Lord is. If you are going to exercise your self unto godliness, you have to know how to exercise your spirit because the very God is in your spirit. These verses are the scriptural ground for the exercise of the spirit.]

B. More Profitable than Bodily Exercise

[In the Greek text of the New Testament, the word for "exercise" is the same as the English word "gymnastics." In the days when the apostle Paul wrote these epistles, gymnastic exercises were practiced by the Greeks. Therefore, the historical background of the word used by Paul was the exercise of bodily gymnastics. Even today, people are learning more and more how to exercise their body for their physical health. However, the apostle Paul utilized this word to stress the vital need of another kind of gymnastics, another kind of exercise that is not related to the physical body. This kind of gymnastics pertains solely to the matter of godliness.

Perhaps some brothers have daily exercises or gymnastics for their body. Well, this is good, for Paul said that bodily exercise has some profit. It is good, but only to a certain degree. However, Paul describes another kind of gymnastics which is good forever—both for today and for eternity! He says that this second kind of gymnastics gives us profit for the life today and for the life in eternity. Therefore, we should pay more attention to this other gymnastics, the exercise of our spirit.]

II. TAKING CARE OF OUR CONSCIENCE

A. A Good Conscience

In order to be able to exercise our spirit it is vital to take care of our conscience. [The conscience is the leading part of our spirit. If our conscience is wrong, we can never have a proper spirit. Moreover, we can never even exercise our spirit. In fact, if our conscience is wrong, our spirit is dead! Therefore, before we can properly exercise our spirit, we must first have a good conscience.]

[If you become contaminated by looking at certain kinds of pictures, your spirit will be defiled, contaminated, and deadened. As a result, you will not be able to pray unless you first ask the Lord to cleanse you from all defilement. I offer this as an illustration of our need to cooperate with the sanctifying Triune God to have our spirit preserved from deadness and contamination.]

B. The Need of the Cleansing Blood

[Therefore, whenever we exercise our spirit to contact the Lord, we need the blood. If we do not know how to apply the blood, we really do not know how to exercise the spirit. Every time we exercise our spirit, we will sense that we need the blood. The cleansing blood is a must; it is absolutely vital and necessary. As soon as we exercise our spirit to contact the Lord, who is righteous and holy, we will sense the need of the blood to cleanse our conscience. He is in the glory, but we are sinful, evil, dirty, worldly and carnal, falling short of His glory! Therefore, the blood must fill the gap between us and the Lord. We must learn to apply the blood constantly.]

III. EXERCISING BY PRAYING

[We have to start to exercise our spirit by praying, because to pray, in principle, is something in the spirit (Eph. 6:18). If you are going to exercise your eyes, you have to see. If you are going to exercise your feet, you have to walk. The more you walk, the more you exercise your feet. In like manner, the best way for you to exercise your spirit is to learn to pray.] However, in your experience it may not seem so easy to pray.

[One reason why we cannot pray is that our spirit has not been used for a long, long time. It is out of function, because it has not been exercised. Once a doctor told me that if we covered our eyes for three months, we would not be able to see. Even though we open our eyes, our sight will be lost, because we have not used our eyes for quite a long time. If we do not use them, our eyes will fail to function. Likewise, many brothers and sisters simply fail to use their spirit. They are constantly using their mind, emotion, will, or their physical body, but not their spirit. Therefore, the spirit fails to function and is consequently lost.]

[The unique way to exercise our spirit is to pray. As we exercise our spirit in prayer, our aim should be to contact the Lord, not first to pray for certain people or things. Simply contact the Lord and allow Him to burden you to pray for certain ones. Do not go to the Lord with your mind filled with things to pray for. If you try to contact the Lord in this way,

144 THE TWO SPIRITS

you will close your spirit. We should come to the Lord with a spirit fully open, worshipping Him, praising Him, and thanking Him. Then we shall know what to pray for, and we shall have much to utter to the Lord in prayer.]

A. Praying Without Ceasing by Calling

[In 1 Thessalonians 5:17 Paul charges us to pray without ceasing. What does it mean to pray unceasingly? Although we may eat several meals a day and although we may drink many times during the day, no one can eat and drink without ceasing. But we certainly breathe unceasingly. Paul's command to pray without ceasing implies that unceasing prayer is like breathing. But how can our prayer become our spiritual breathing? How can we turn prayer into breathing? The way to do this is to call on the name of the Lord. We need to call on the Lord Jesus continually. This is the way to breathe, to pray without ceasing. Because we are not accustomed to this, we need to practice calling on the Lord's name all the time. To live is to breathe. Spiritually speaking, to breathe is to call on the Lord's name and to pray. By calling on the name of the Lord Jesus, we breathe the Spirit.]

B. Pray-reading the Word

As we have seen in Lesson Twelve, the Spirit is embodied in the Word. In order to experience the supply of the Spirit in the Word we must exercise our spirit. Pray-reading is one of the best ways to exercise our spirit.

[Let us use Psalm 133 to show the difference between analyzing the Bible and enjoying the nourishment contained in it by pray-reading. In their time of personal devotions, some Christians may read Psalm 133. As they read, they may begin to analyze and to ask about the precious ointment, the beard, the skirts, the dew, and Mount Hermon. Instead of receiving the bountiful supply, they are left with many unanswered questions. But if we pray-read Psalm 133, we shall take this portion in the way of life. As we pray-read, we may say, "Behold, amen! How good and how pleasant, amen." By taking the Word in this way, we shall apply the all-inclusive

Spirit to our inner being. By pray-reading we exercise our spirit to receive spiritual nourishment from the Word. Through this nourishment we grow in life. We are nourished with the words of faith and healthy teaching. If we take even as little as ten minutes to pray-read a portion of the Word, we shall receive nourishment. Furthermore, we shall experience the various elements of Christ's riches.]

IV. EXERCISING OUR SPIRIT IN THE MEETINGS

Finally, we must see that it is crucial to exercise our spirit in the church meetings. [Whenever we Christians come together in a church meeting, we need to function. We need to pray, praise, or give a word of testimony. This is to exercise our spirit and not allow it to remain dormant or in a deadened condition. But sorry to say, many saints do not preserve their spirit by exercising it in this way. Instead, they allow their spirit to remain dormant. It seems that they leave their spirit in a tomb.]

[When everyone exercises his spirit in a meeting, the Holy Spirit is free to move and flow. But this is a real battle, for Satan knows that if we all release our spirits, he will be defeated. He subtly hits the strategic point of choking the spirit of the saints. As long as he can choke our spirit, we are finished and he is successful. Therefore, we must fight the battle. We must learn to practice releasing our spirit all the time and be continually ready to pray. Whenever we come to a meeting, we must immediately exercise and release our spirit to pray.]

[All our problems are solved and all our needs are met through the exercise of our spirit. All that God is and all that He has accomplished are in the all-inclusive Spirit who has been installed in our spirit. Therefore, by turning to our spirit and by exercising our spirit, we may obtain the full supply to meet our need.]

SUMMARY

We believers must know how to exercise our spirit to contact the Lord. In order to exercise our spirit we must take care of our conscience by applying the cleansing blood. The unique way to exercise our spirit is to pray. We can all pray without ceasing by calling on the name of the Lord continually. We exercise our spirit to receive spiritual nourishment from the Word by pray-reading. We must exercise our spirit in the church meetings by praying, praising, or giving a word of testimony.

Questions

1. How did Paul relate bodily exercise to our spirit? In what verse do we find this?

2. Why is exercising our spirit more profitable than bodily exercise?

3. In exercising our spirit, why do we need to first take care of our conscience?

4. What is the best way to exercise our spirit?

5. In what way can we pray unceasingly?

Quoted Portions
from (Lee/LSM) Publications

1. *Our Human Spirit,* p. 70.

2. *The Stream, Vol. 5, No. 1, February 1, 1967*pp. 3, 10-11.

3. *Life-study of First Thessalonians,* p. 208.

4. *The Stream, Vol. 5, No. 1, February 1, 1967,*p. 22.

5. *Our Human Spirit,* p. 72.

6. *The Stream, Vol. 5, No. 1, February 1, 1967,*p. 33.

7. *Life-study of Colossians,* p. 423.

8. *Life-study of Philippians,* pp. 298, 319-320.

9. *Life-study of First Thessalonians,* p. 204.

10. *The Stream, Vol. 5, No. 1, February 1, 1967,*p. 27.

11. *Life-study of Romans,* p. 589.

WALKING ACCORDING TO SPIRIT AND TWO WALKS BY THE SPIRIT

Scripture Reading

Rom. 8:4, 16; 1 Cor. 6:17; Rom. 8:14; Gal. 5:16, 22-23, 25

Outline

I. Walking according to spirit
II. Being led by the Spirit
III. Two kinds of walk by the Spirit
    A. Walking about—the first walk
    B. Walking in line—the second walk
    C. Walking by the Spirit as the rule

Text

I. WALKING ACCORDING TO SPIRIT

[If you read through your Bible, going on from the Old Testament through to the end of the New Testament, you will see that the Lord's ultimate charge to you is not that you follow laws or teachings, but that you walk according to spirit.]

[In Romans 8:4 we are told to walk, not according to the flesh, but according to the spirit. The spirit here in Romans 8:4 is the mingled spirit, our spirit mingled with the Holy Spirit (Rom. 8:16; 1 Cor. 6:17). We have to walk according to our spirit because today the Holy Spirit is within our spirit and is even one with our spirit. When we walk according to our spirit, spontaneously we walk according to the Holy Spirit, because the two spirits are one.

Most people walk and do things according to the mind, according to what they think, and according to what they like. Some who walk according to the flesh are doing sinful things, while others are doing good things according to their mind, their thinking, and their likes and dislikes. But we Christians should walk according to the spirit. It is easy to discern the spirit from the flesh, but sometimes it is not easy to discern the spirit from the mind. Perhaps, for example, you may be thinking about visiting a brother, but deep within something is bothering you. You should walk not according to your thinking or your likes and dislikes, but just according to the "inner red light" or the "inner green light." This is to walk according to your spirit.]

[To walk means to live, to act, or to have one's being. We must live and act and have our being, not according to the Ten Commandments, or the so-called Sermon on the Mount, or some doctrines, but according to the mingled spirit.

Practice walking this way. Every day, from morning till evening, cease from your doing and seek to constantly remain in this mingled spirit.]

II. BEING LED BY THE SPIRIT

[Romans 8:14 says, "For as many as are led by the Spirit of God, these are sons of God." This verse is a continuation of the foregoing portion in which Paul tells us that we must walk according to spirit (v. 4). In a sense, to walk according to spirit is to be under the leading of the Holy Spirit.]

[The inward life gives you the sense, even in small things, of whether or not you are under the Lord's leading. Thus, we are led of the Spirit by walking according to spirit and by setting our mind upon the spirit. Therefore, the leading of the Spirit mentioned in verse 14 is not derived from the outward environment, but from the inward sense and consciousness of the divine life. This leading proves that we are sons of God, for "as many as are led by the Spirit of God, these are sons of God."

I would like to say a word especially to the teenagers who might be reading this message. While your classmates are talking in a worldly way, you may find yourself, at a certain point, unable to join in the conversation. Although nothing outward frustrates you, you do sense an inner forbidding. This inward regulation comes from the life of God within you, the life which makes you a child of God. Your classmates may be discussing sinful things in a happy, excited way, but the divine life within you does not allow you to say a word. Instead, it turns you away from them. That is the leading of the Spirit. This leading of the Spirit marks you out as a son of God. Because of this mark from the leading of the Spirit your classmates will wonder what has happened to you. They will wonder why you do not talk and what is different about you. They will wonder because they are sons of the devil and you are a son of God. You have the leading of the Spirit within you.]

III. TWO KINDS OF WALK BY THE SPIRIT

[In Galatians 5 Paul speaks twice about walking by the Spirit.]

A. Walking About—the First Walk

[The Greek word for *walk* in verse 16, *peripateo,* means to have our being, to deport ourselves, to order our manner of life, to walk about. It is used with respect to ordinary daily life. It denotes a common, habitual daily walk. This understanding of walking by the Spirit is confirmed by verses 22 and 23, where Paul speaks of the fruit of the Spirit. The various aspects of the fruit of the Spirit mentioned in these verses are not unusual things; they are aspects of our ordinary daily life. Therefore, the walk in verse 16 is our habitual and common daily walk.]

B. Walking in Line—the Second Walk

[The Greek word for *walk* in verse 25, *stoicheo,* has a very different meaning. It is derived from a root which means to arrange in a line. This may be illustrated by the movement of traffic in designated lanes on a highway. Thus, the Greek word for walk here means to walk in line. It also means to march in military rank. Walking in this way, like soldiers marching in rank, requires that we keep in step.

As we compare these two kinds of walk, we see that the second is more regulated than the first. In the second walk we need to walk like an army and keep in step, whereas in the first kind of walk we are free to walk about. However, both kinds of walk, the common, ordinary walk and the walking in line or in rank, are by the Spirit.]

[In our daily living as Christians, we need to have two kinds of walk by the Spirit. The first is a general walk, whereas the second is the walk according to a certain rule or principle for the fulfillment of God's eternal purpose. In the first kind of walk, we need to display the fruit of the Spirit, the virtues listed in 5:22 and 23. However, we are not here simply to exhibit such virtues as love, joy, and peace. We are here for the fulfillment of God's purpose. Thus, we need to walk according to certain rules or principles for the fulfillment of this purpose. For God's purpose, we need to have a walk that is orderly, a walk that is according to certain elementary rules or basic principles. Loving and being joyful are not basic rules or principles. These are simply different aspects of our daily life as Christians, not the characteristics of the walk which leads to the fulfillment of God's purpose. This walk, the second kind of walk by the Spirit, requires that we walk according to basic principles and elementary rules.

We may use the daily life of a young sister who is a student to illustrate the two kinds of walk by the Spirit. On the one hand, this sister lives with her family at home. If she truly lives Christ, she will show forth the virtues of Christ to the members of her family. On the other hand, she needs to be a proper student at school and fulfill all the requirements leading to graduation. At home she needs to walk as a daughter and sister, but at school she needs to walk as a proper student. She needs to have both the general walk at home with her family and the more specific walk at school according to basic rules and elementary principles.]

C. Walking by the Spirit as the Rule

[If we consider Galatians 5:25 in light of the other verses where the Greek word *stoicheo* is used for *walk* (Rom. 4:12; Phil. 3:16), we shall see that to walk by the Spirit is to walk by the Spirit as our rule. The Spirit Himself is the way, the rule, the line, the principle, leading toward God's goal. The Spirit Himself should be our rule. If we would have the second walk by the Spirit, we must take the Spirit as our rule, our way. This may be illustrated by driving on the highway to reach a specific destination, which is different from merely driving around. When we drive on the highway, the lanes on the highway are a rule. Driving according to this rule, we are able to reach our destination.

In our Christian walk, the second kind of walk by the Spirit is a walk in which the Spirit is the rule. Our rule should not be doctrine or theology. Furthermore, it should not be the law. Paul's intention in writing to the Galatians was to tell them that they should no longer take the law as their rule. The Galatian believers had been distracted from the Spirit to the law and had taken it as their rule. Paul told them that they were foolish and that they should return to the Spirit as their rule. Since they had life and lived by the Spirit, they should also walk by the Spirit as their rule. If we would have the second walk for the fulfillment of God's purpose, we must first learn to walk by the Spirit as our way, rule, principle, and lane.

I encourage all the saints to have the second walk by the Spirit. You need to pray, "Lord, I will follow You to have the second walk by the Spirit for the fulfillment of Your purpose. I do not want to walk by doctrine, theology, organization, or natural concepts. I want to walk by the Spirit as my unique highway."

According to 5:25, since we have received life and live by the Spirit, we should now have the second walk by the Spirit as our rule. We have been given life by the Spirit that we may walk by the Spirit to fulfill God's purpose. What a glorious goal lies before us! The highway which leads us to this goal is the Spirit, the ultimate expression of the processed Triune God. As we walk on this unique highway, we should neither swerve nor turn around, but move on directly to the goal.]

SUMMARY

The Lord's ultimate charge is that we live, act, and have our being according to the spirit. We are led by the Spirit by walking according to the inward sense of the divine life. Two kinds of walk by the spirit are mentioned in Galatians 5. The first walk is a general daily walk displaying such virtues as love, joy and peace. The second walk is according to certain elementary rules and principles for the fulfillment of God's purpose. We should live by the Spirit and have the second walk by the Spirit as our rule.

Questions

1. When we say "walk according to spirit," what do we mean by the word "walk"?

2. How does the inner sense of life help us walk by the spirit?

3. What verses in Galatians show us the two walks by the spirit?

4. Define the Greek words *peripateo* and *stoicheo*.

5. Explain the difference between the two walks in Galatians 5.

Quoted Portions
from (Lee/LSM) Publications

1. *Life Messages,* pp. 431-432.

2. *Our Human Spirit,* p. 38.

3. *Life Messages,* p. 432.

4. *Life-study of Romans,* pp. 215, 222-223.

5. *Life-study of Galatians,* pp. 333-334, 375, 349-350.

Lesson Twenty-One

SERVING IN OUR SPIRIT

Scripture Reading

Rom. 1:9; 7:6; 12:1, 11; 2 Cor. 3:6, 8

Outline

I. Life and service
II. The service being the ministering of Christ
III. The basis of our service
    A. By the growth in life
    B. In the Body
    C. In the spirit
       1. Not in oldness of letter
       2. In newness of our regenerated spirit
IV. Ministering Christ in the practical service

Text

The apostle Paul said in Romans 1:9, "For God is my witness, whom I serve in my spirit in the gospel of His Son, how unceasingly I make mention of you always in my prayers." Then he said in Romans 7:6, "But now we are discharged from the law, having died to that in which we were held, that we should serve as slaves in newness of spirit and not in oldness of letter." He begged us, "therefore, brothers, through the compassions of God to present your bodies a living sacrifice, holy, well-pleasing to God, which is your most reasonable service" (Rom. 12:1). He also charged us not to be slothful in zeal, but to be burning in spirit, serving the Lord as a slave" (Rom. 12:11).

I. LIFE AND SERVICE

In this lesson [we are dealing with the practical aspect of the Christian life, that is, the service. With us as Christians there are always two aspects. The first aspect is a matter of the Christian life, a life matter, and the second aspect is a

matter of the Christian service, a service matter. As the
Lord's children, on the one hand we need a proper life, a spiritual life, and on the other hand we need a proper service, a
spiritual service.

In Matthew 25 the Lord Jesus gave two parables, the
parable of the ten virgins, which deals with the Christian life,
and the parable of the talents, which is related to our service.
As far as our life is concerned, we should be as the virgins
with the testimony of light in our hand as we go out of this
world to meet our Bridegroom. This is our life, the life aspect.
We need the oil, and we need the testimony of light. We need
to go out of this world, to wait for the Lord's coming back,
and to go on to meet His coming. This is the Christian life.

Immediately following this parable, the Lord gave us the
parable of the talents, which is something related to our
service. We need to use the talent, the gift, which the Lord has
given us, to do some business and to make some profit for the
Lord. With the Lord's children there are always these two
aspects, the life and the service. We need to grow in life with
the oil, with the light, and with the going out of this world to
meet the Lord in His coming back. We also need to exercise in
a proper way what the Lord has given us as a gift, as a
talent.]

II. THE SERVICE BEING THE MINISTERING
OF CHRIST

The service we are talking about is certainly not the
so-called "Sunday morning service" to which many Christians
are accustomed. Neither is it just to perform some work such
as cleaning the church meeting hall, although that can be
part of serving. The real service is our functioning in the
church life in a way that ministers Christ. In preaching
the gospel, offering a prayer, or giving a testimony in the
meeting, you should have the view that you are serving
Christ to others. A stewardess on an airplane serves people
with refreshments. Similarly, in the church we should be ones
who serve people with Christ.

[To minister Christ as life to others should be the purpose
of all the things we do, whether we are cleaning, arranging,

cooking, visiting, ministering the Word, singing, or praying. All the practical things in the church life are nothing but the channels, the means through which, by which, and in which we would minister Christ to others.

If others cannot sense Christ in the kitchen while you are cooking, it is doubtful that they will sense Him in the meetings in a real way. To have Christ ministered in the meetings we need to exercise ourselves in such a way in doing all the practical things that Christ will be ministered in the practical things. Every part of the service of the church must minister Christ as life.

We need to learn to serve in the spirit, and we need to learn to do all the things in the service of the church in a way that ministers Christ to others. This is our aim and purpose.]

III. THE BASIS OF OUR SERVICE

A. By the Growth in Life

[First we have the aspect of life, then the aspect of service. We have the life matter settled first, then, based on that fact, we have the matter of service. Without life and the adequate growth in life, we cannot have the service. The little children can do many things, but they cannot serve, because they simply do not have the adequate growth in life.]

In the foregoing lessons we have covered many aspects and practices of life that can help you to grow in life. We must all rise up to serve according to our capacity in life. We should not excuse ourselves as being too young. Every believer should have a proper life of service.

B. In the Body

[The Christian service is a matter of life and in the Body. It is a matter in the Body and a matter of the Body. You cannot serve the Lord as an individual Christian. To serve the Lord, you need to realize that the Lord's service is something in the Body.

Every believer is a member of the Body, a part of the Body. An individual is not the Body. A member of the Body cannot function without the Body. The hand is good, quite useful, but if it is cut off from the body, it becomes not only dead, but also ugly, terrible, and even terrifying. You may love to shake my hand, but if this hand were detached from the body, it would be terrible.

Today many Christians are detached, separated from the reality of the Body. It is as if they are disembodied members. The members of the body are beautiful as long as they are attached where they belong in the body, but in any other place they are terrible. How sad it is that many Christians today are like ears that have been detached and put on the shoulders. How could they serve the Lord? How could we serve the Lord without being built up together as members of the Body? It is impossible.]

C. In the Spirit

1. Not in Oldness of Letter

[Now we come to a crucial point; that is, we need to learn how to serve in the spirit. Romans 7:6 says, "But now we are discharged from the law, having died to that in which we were held, that we should serve in newness of spirit and not in oldness of letter." We need to learn to serve in the spirit—not in the letter, not in the law, not in doctrine, but in the spirit.

Second Corinthians 3:6 indicates that the New Testament service is a matter of the Spirit, not of the letter: "Who also made us sufficient as ministers of a new covenant, not of letter, but of the Spirit; for the letter kills, but the Spirit gives life." Verse 8 continues, "How shall not rather the ministry of the Spirit be in glory?"]

2. In Newness of Our Regenerated Spirit

[I am afraid that many believers simply do not know what it means to serve in the spirit. Before we were saved, we were dead in our spirit. On one hand, we were very active in the mind and in the emotion; yet we were dead in the spirit. But, praise the Lord, at the time we were saved, the Lord regenerated our spirit and made it alive. From that time, we need to learn to live, to walk, to act in the spirit, not in the mind or emotion, not in the soul.

We need to learn not only to walk, to live, in the spirit but also to serve in the spirit, and to serve in the newness of the spirit. My burden is to help you know something in a practical way, not in the way of doctrine or theory.

What does it mean to serve the Lord in the spirit and in the newness of the spirit? A spirit has been created within us, and we have been regenerated. Our spirit has been renewed, and the Spirit of God is now dwelling in this quickened, renewed spirit. Therefore our spirit is now a strong factor in our being. Because this spirit has been renewed and made alive, and because it has been strengthened by the indwelling of the Holy Spirit, it surely is a strong factor in our being. Yet, due to the fact that we lack the proper teaching, we simply do not realize that we have such a renewed spirit with the Holy Spirit indwelling it. However, we should have some realization because of all the speaking in the ministry concerning this matter.

On one hand, we need to walk, to live, in this spirit. We are not speaking of the Holy Spirit, but of our renewed spirit in which the Holy Spirit dwells. To walk, to live, in our spirit means that we will be in the Holy Spirit because the Holy Spirit is now indwelling our spirit. We need to live in the spirit, and we need to learn to serve in the spirit.]

IV. MINISTERING CHRIST
IN THE PRACTICAL SERVICE

[The purpose of all we do in the church service is to minister Christ to others. Everything we do should minister life to others.

Suppose you come to the meeting hall to take care of some practical matters, to arrange the chairs, to do some cleaning work, or to take care of the kitchen. Whatever you are doing, you should take that as an opportunity to minister Christ to others. If you are cleaning, your cleaning should minister life to others. You need to minister Christ by cleaning. If you are teaching, your teaching should minister life to others. Merely to minister some knowledge to others is not enough. You need to minister Christ by teaching. It is the same with cooking. Even by cooking you should minister Christ.]

[There are many lessons to learn in ministering Christ to others by cleaning, by cooking, and by doing many different practical things. It seems that we are so spiritual, so Christ-like, when we come together for a meeting, but when we are in the kitchen it seems that we are anything but Christ-like. We need to learn the lesson to serve others and to serve God by ministering Christ to others no matter what we are doing. If you are in the spirit when you are playing the piano, by playing the piano you will minister Christ to others. As the church we are here to do nothing else but minister Christ to others. To cook a good meal for the saints, to prepare a good place for meeting, to play the piano in a skillful way— none of these things are meaningful unless they minister Christ to others. Whatever we do in the service of the Lord should minister Christ to others. We have much to learn in this matter.]

SUMMARY

There are two aspects of being a Christian: one is of life and the other is of service. We need to have a proper spiritual service as well as the growth in life. The real service is to minister Christ in whatever we do, whether it is gospel preaching or cleaning the meeting hall. Our serving should be by the growth in life, in the Body, and in our regenerated spirit.

Questions

1. Explain how the parables of the virgins and the talents in Matthew 25 show the aspects of life and service.

2. What is the real church service?

3. Since the real service is the ministering of Christ, can you see why our serving is based firstly on the growth in life?

4. Why is serving a matter of the Body?

5. What has happened to our once dead spirit that makes it possible for us to serve in newness of spirit?

Quoted Portions
from (Lee/LSM) Publications

1. *To Serve in the Human Spirit,* pp. 78-79, 99-100, 80-81, 90-91, 97-99.

THE TRIUNE GOD AS THE SPIRIT
SATURATING THE TRIPARTITE MAN

Scripture Reading

Rom. 8:1-11; John 14:10-11; 1 Cor. 15:45b; 1 Thes. 5:22

Outline

I. The Triune God
   A. Revealed in Romans eight
   B. Three-one
II. The tripartite man
   A. Body and soul and spirit
   B. The spirit making man unique
   C. Regenerated with the divine seed
III. The imparting of life to every part of our being
   A. Our spirit being life
   B. Our soul becoming life
   C. Life imparted to our mortal bodies
   D. Our whole being saturated with God
IV. The need to see the vision

Text

I. THE TRIUNE GOD

A. Revealed in Romans Eight

[The Spirit that we are referring to is *the* Spirit; that is, it is the Triune God who has been processed and has become the life-giving Spirit. This Triune God, as our title says, saturates the tripartite man. Look at Romans 8:9, and you will see the reference to the Triune God. "But you are not in the flesh, but in the spirit, if indeed the Spirit of God dwells in you. But if any one has not the Spirit of Christ, he is not of Him." Notice that God, Christ, and the Spirit are all mentioned here. Yet this verse is not making a doctrinal statement; it is dealing with our experience. Contrary to the way Christianity presents it, the Trinity is not a doctrine for us to subscribe to. We need God to be triune in order that we may experience Him. God, Christ, and the Spirit are all in our experience.]

B. Three-One

[John 14 clearly says that the Son is in the Father and the Father in the Son (vv. 10-11). To see the Son is to see the Father. When the Son speaks, it is the Father who is working. The Two are inseparable. The Bible goes on to say that the Son, after death and resurrection, became the Spirit (1 Cor. 15:45b). The Son, in whom is the Father, has become the Spirit. Thus, the Triune God can come into the sinner. With the Spirit comes the Son; when the Son comes, the Father comes as well.

The term triune means three in one. From one side there are three; but from the other side they are one, because they cannot be separated.

Notice the three terms Paul uses in Romans 8:9 and 10. He says *the Spirit of God* dwells in you; that without *the Spirit of Christ* you are not of Him; that *Christ* is in you. Why does Paul use three terms to refer to the same One? It is because this One has three aspects: the aspects of the Father, of the Son, and of the Spirit.]

II. TRIPARTITE MAN

[Not only is God triune; man is tripartite. We human beings are spirit, soul, and body. We were created in this way, so that we could be organically grafted to God, and so that the two spirits, His and ours, could be joined together.]

A. Body and Soul and Spirit

[Man, as we have often pointed out, can be represented by three concentric circles. The outer ring corresponds to our physical body, the part of us that has substance and can be seen and touched. Besides this part, we have a soul, represented by the middle ring. This is the psychological part of us, enabling us to think, to love or hate, and to make decisions. The soul, then, consists of the mind, the emotion, and the will.

The innermost ring, the deepest part of man, is the spirit. You may not be clear about the human spirit, but one part of it, the conscience, you are familiar with. The conscience is deeper than the mind, emotion, and will.]

B. The Spirit Making Man Unique

[Such is the way man is made. Animals may have a part that corresponds to the soul, but they lack this inner part, man's worshipping organ. There has never been a case in the whole history where a donkey, or a monkey, or a goat built a little sanctuary and set up an image to worship! The record of mankind, in contrast, is replete with religions, idols, temples, and forms of worship. Cultured or barbarian, ancient or modern—all peoples have a desire to worship a higher Being. What accounts for this difference between man and the animals? What constrains man to worship? It is because man was made by God with a spirit.]

C. Regenerated with the Divine Seed

[What is the distinction between an unregenerated human being and a believer? Both have these three parts of body, soul, and spirit. The believer, however, has a divine seed in his spirit. The seed of God abides in him!]

[This seed of the divine life and nature needs to grow. As it grows, it develops and spreads from the spirit into the soul, especially into the mind, the leading part of the soul. If we allow this seed to grow without hindrance, it will spread even to our mortal body.]

III. THE IMPARTING OF LIFE
TO EVERY PART OF OUR BEING

[In 8:1-11 we see that, after having passed through the various processes, the Triune God became a life-giving Spirit, the Spirit who gives life. In verse 11 Paul clearly says that the One who raised Christ from among the dead gives life to our mortal bodies "through His Spirit Who indwells you." This Spirit now dwells in our spirit.]

A. Our Spirit Being Life

[As the life-giving Spirit, the processed Triune God dwells in us to give us life in a threefold way. The first aspect of this giving of life is found in verse 10: "And if Christ is in you, though the body is dead because of sin, yet the spirit is life because of righteousness." This verse says that if Christ is in us, our spirit is life. Christ here is the very Triune God who has become the indwelling Spirit. Because this Christ is in us, our spirit is life, for as the life-giving Spirit, Christ dwells in our spirit, and His indwelling makes our spirit life. This is the first aspect of the giving of life revealed in Romans 8.]

B. Our Soul Becoming Life

[The second aspect is found in verse 6: "For the mind set on the flesh is death, but the mind set on the spirit is life and peace." The mind is the leading part of our soul. As such, it represents our soul. This means that when the mind becomes life, our soul becomes life. First our spirit is life, and then our soul also becomes life.]

[In whatever we do and say, we must be sure that our mind is on our spirit. When our mind is off our spirit, we are like an electrical appliance which has been disconnected. If we sense that our mind is not on our spirit, we should stop and call on the name of the Lord Jesus. Many of us can testify that after simply calling on the name of the Lord Jesus, we had the sense deep within that, once again, our mind was on our spirit. Although this is simple matter, it is very serious.]

C. Life Imparted to Our Mortal Bodies

[Finally, life is imparted to our mortal bodies. According to verse 11, He who raised Christ Jesus from among the dead gives life to our mortal bodies through the indwelling Spirit.]

[If we allow the indwelling Spirit to make His home in our being, this indwelling Spirit will saturate our dying, mortal body with resurrection life. Our mortal body will be enlivened, quickened, and healed with the divine life.]

[Therefore, life is imparted to us in a threefold way: Our spirit becomes life, our mind becomes life, and life is imparted to our mortal bodies. For this reason we can say that, according to Romans 8, the Triune God is dispensed into the tripartite man and gives life to man's spirit, soul, and body.]

D. Our Whole Being Saturated with God

> Thy Spirit will me saturate,
> Every part will God permeate....

Hymns, #501

[Our relationship with God should reach to this extent. Our whole being must be saturated with Him. We should not be content with outwardly worshipping Him, loving Him, fearing Him, and doing things to please Him. This mysterious God has passed through a process: creation, incarnation, human living, death, resurrection, and ascension. Now He has returned as the Spirit to enter all who believe in Him. Such is our God and our Savior.

He does not want us to worship Him from afar. He does not want us to stand in awe of Him. Nor does He want us to perform certain duties to please Him. What He wants is that we open the deepest part of our being to Him and call on His name. Then His Spirit comes into us, making our deadened spirit life. From there He spreads out. As we set our mind on the spirit, the soul too is saturated with Him. It also becomes life. From the soul, life spreads also to our mortal body. The resurrection life saturates it. When every part of us is saturated with this all-inclusive life-giving Spirit, we are in the union that God wants.]

IV. THE NEED TO SEE THE VISION

[We all need to see the vision of the dispensing of the life of the Triune God into the three parts of our being. If we see this divine vision, our natural concept of ethics and morality will be shattered. We need to say to the Lord, "Lord, I thank You. Since You came into me, my spirit has become life. Now if I set my mind on my spirit, my mind also will be life. O Lord, how I praise You! Through Your indwelling Spirit, Your *zoe* (Greek, *God's divine life*) life can be dispensed even into my mortal body. Lord, I worship You for this, I enjoy this, and I am one with You in this dispensation." This is the dispensation of the life of the Triune God into the tripartite man. Through such a dispensing the Triune God becomes one with the tripartite man, and the tripartite man becomes one with the Triune God. It is through this dispensation of the divine life that we become sons of God. Furthermore, it is by this dispensation that we are transformed and conformed to the image of Christ. This is the Christian life and the church life.]

SUMMARY

Romans eight reveals the Triune God dispensing Himself into the tripartite man. The Triune God as the Spirit enters into man's spirit making it life. As the mind is set on the spirit, the mind becomes life and eventually life is given even to our mortal bodies. Thus, the Triune God as the Spirit fully saturates the tripartite man, making God and man fully one.

Questions

1. Explain how we can see the Triune God in Romans 8.

2. Of how many parts is man composed? Name them.

3. What distinguishes man from other creatures?

4. Explain how the Triune God dwells in us to give us life in a threefold way.

Quoted Portions
from (Lee/LSM) Publications

1. *Life Messages*, pp. 516-518, 710-711.

2. *Life-study of Romans*, pp. 696-697.

3. *Life-study of Hebrews*, p. 728.

4. *Life-study of Romans*, p. 697.

5. *Life-study of John*, p. 160.

6. *Life-study of Romans*, p. 697.

7. *Life Messages*, p. 519.

8. *Life-study of Romans*, pp. 652-653.

Lesson Twenty-Three

THE BODY OF CHRIST
AND OUR REGENERATED SPIRIT

Scripture Reading

Eph. 1:17; 2:22; 3:16; 4:23; Rom. 8:6;
Col. 1:19; 2:9; Eph. 6:18

Outline

I. The Body of Christ and our regenerated spirit in
Ephesians
II. A spirit of revelation to see the Body
III. Built together in spirit
IV. Strengthened in the inner man
V. Renewed in the spirit of the mind
VI. Filled in spirit
VII. Praying in spirit

Text

[The reason there is virtually no church life in Christianity today is that most Christians do not know the human spirit. Rather, most of today's Christian teachings are concerned with the mind. The book of Ephesians, however, is not focused on the mind, but on the spirit. Our spirit must be a spirit of wisdom and revelation, the place of God's building, the organ in which God reveals His mystery to us, and the inner man strengthened by the Spirit of God. Furthermore, we need to be renewed in the spirit of our mind and to pray in spirit. Through proper exercise, our spirit will eventually be filled unto all the fullness of God. This is the mingling of God and man that produces the church life.]

I. THE BODY OF CHRIST
AND OUR REGENERATED SPIRIT IN EPHESIANS

[First of all, we need to see that the Body is a matter absolutely in the spirit, in our human spirit. Our regenerated spirit is indwelt by the Holy Spirit, but the emphasis with the Body of Christ today is on our human spirit rather than on the Holy Spirit. Therefore, in every chapter of the book of Ephesians there is something mentioned about our regenerated human spirit. Ephesians is a book on the Body, and every chapter contains a verse concerning the human spirit. We need to pray-read these verses again and again.]

II. A SPIRIT OF REVELATION
TO SEE THE BODY

[Paul prayed that the Father of glory "may give to you a spirit of wisdom and revelation" (Eph. 1:17). The spirit here is our regenerated spirit indwelt by the Spirit of God. It is necessary for you to see the Body, but you could never see the Body unless you are in the spirit. If you do not have the vision in your spirit, if you do not have a spirit of revelation, a seeing spirit, you could not see the Body. If your eyes do not have sight, you could not distinguish one color from another, and you could not view the scenery. The Body of Christ is something different from all the scenes we could see, something different from all the colors we could see naturally. It is a heavenly vision. Therefore, we need a spirit of revelation, a spirit of seeing, a seeing spirit, to see the Body. I do not mean that we need a clever mind to understand. What we need is a spirit transparent to see, a spirit of revelation, a seeing spirit to see the Body. The spirit of revelation to see the Body is the first point concerning our spirit in this book on the church.]

[To use our mind to try to understand the matter of the church instead of turning to our spirit to see the revelation of the church can be compared to trying to see a particular color with our eyes closed instead of opening our eyes to see that color. With your eyes closed, without the faculty of vision, you cannot see any of the colors. The faculty of understanding does not work for the colors. But if you open your eyes, all the doubts are gone, all the questions are gone, and you do know what the particular color is. You may not be able to explain what you see, but your eyes can substantiate the colors and can distinguish one color from another. To see the colors, we need to open our eyes. To see the church, we need to turn to our spirit. We need to turn to our spirit and respect the fact that our spirit is a spirit of revelation. To see the church is simple when you use the proper organ. In the spirit the matter of the church is very clear. The local church is different from all the denominations. You may not be able to explain the difference, but when you turn to the spirit and see the church, you will know the difference, and you will know that you have seen the church.]

III. BUILT TOGETHER IN SPIRIT

[The matter of seeing the church is in the spirit, and the building up of the church is also in the spirit. In Ephesians 2:22 Paul says that "you also are being built together into a dwelling place of God in spirit." As long as we stay outside of the spirit, we are divided, and we are also divisive. As long as we are not in the spirit, we are individualistic. It is not at all hard to be divisive or to be individualistic. Simply by staying away from our spirit, simply by lingering in our mind to consider or by lingering in our emotion, we are divisive, we are individualistic, and we are not willing to be tempered. We have our likes and dislikes, our tastes and preferences, our opinions about the brothers and sisters, and we would rather stay at home than be in the meetings with the saints. As long as we stay away from our spirit, we see no need to be tempered together, and we feel it is necessary for each of us to maintain a distinctiveness from others, to take care of our individual personality created by God, and to hold on to our own prestige. It is impossible for us to be tempered together as long as we stay outside the spirit with such concepts. However, if we would turn ourselves to the spirit, right away we would see that we need to be tempered, we would be willing to be tempered, and we would even cry out to the Lord for His mercy that He would temper us together.]

IV. STRENGTHENED IN THE INNER MAN

[Furthermore, we need to be strengthened in the inner man, in our regenerated human spirit. In chapter three of

Ephesians Paul prayed, "That He would grant you, according to the riches of His glory, to be strengthened with power through His Spirit into the inner man" (v. 16). Not only is the seeing of the Body in the spirit, not only is the building up together of the Body in the spirit, but the strengthening in the inner man is also in the spirit. In order to be strengthened in the inner man we need to be in the spirit. We are too strong in the emotion, in the will, and in the mind, but we are not strong enough in the inner man, in the spirit. We need to be strengthened in the inner man. The strengthening of God is in our spirit.]

V. RENEWED IN THE SPIRIT OF THE MIND

[Then in chapter four of Ephesians, after the strengthening in the inner man, there is the renewing of the spirit of the mind (v. 23). Every part of your mind needs to be completely renewed, renewed in the spirit that takes over, occupies, and possesses your mind and becomes the spirit of your mind. You may not realize how much your mind controls your spirit and even controls the Holy Spirit. Without the cooperation of your mind, the Holy Spirit could not get through in you. In this sense, the Holy Spirit is under the control of your mind. However, this is not the proper order. Both the Holy Spirit and our human spirit should be over our mind and should take full control of our mind. The mind should be set upon the spirit (Rom. 8:6), and the mind should be governed, possessed, occupied, taken over, controlled, and subdued by the spirit. Then this spirit is the renewing spirit.

All of us need to be renewed again and again, daily, hourly, moment by moment, all the time, in, with, and by such a renewing spirit. If such is the case, the local church life will be real and precious to you, and you will realize that there is no other way for you to go on, no other way for you to take.]

VI. FILLED IN SPIRIT

[In the first four chapters of Ephesians there is the seeing in the spirit (1:17), building up in the spirit (2:22), being strengthened in the spirit (3:16), and being renewed in the spirit (4:23). In chapter five Paul indicates that we need to be filled in spirit. According to 3:19, to be filled in spirit means to be filled unto all the fullness of the Godhead. When Christ makes His home in our heart, and when we are strong to apprehend with all the saints the dimensions of Christ and to know by experience His knowledge-surpassing love, we shall be filled unto all the fullness of God. All this fullness dwells in Christ (Col. 1:19; 2:9). Through His indwelling, Christ imparts what God is into our being. We can be filled with God to such a measure and standard, even unto all the fullness of God.]

[It seems that we often are full in our mind, but empty in the spirit. Our spirit seems somewhat like a flat tire, but our mind and emotion are both filled up. We need to pray that we would be emptied in the mind and emptied in the emotion, but filled unto the fullness of God in our spirit. Then the church life will be very valuable to us. We will treasure the church life.]

VII. PRAYING IN SPIRIT

[Finally, in chapter six of Ephesians, Paul says that we need to pray at every time in spirit (v. 18). This prayer is the prayer of a member of the Body identified with Christ on the throne, all the time claiming, proclaiming, giving command to the Lord, and binding the enemy. This is not the prayer of a beggar, not begging prayer, not the prayer of the poor sinner, not the prayer of the poor, weak saints pleading with the Lord, but the prayer of the Body, the prayer of members of the Body identified with the Head.]

[We need to see the Body in the spirit, to be built up in the spirit, to be strengthened in the spirit, to be renewed in the spirit, to be filled unto the fullness of God in the spirit, and to pray in spirit as members of the Body, identified with the Head. If such is the case, spontaneously we will have the church life. If not, it will be hard to have the church life. We may have a lot of talk about the Body life and a lot of teachings about the church, but we will have no way at all to realize what the church life actually is. I urge you again and again to turn to the spirit because the church life is in your spirit.]

SUMMARY

The Body of Christ is a matter absolutely in spirit, in our human spirit. In order to see the Body, we need a spirit of wisdom and revelation. The building up of the church is also in spirit. Furthermore, in order to be strengthened into the inner man, we need to be in spirit. We need to be renewed in the spirit of our mind, and we need to pray in spirit. Through the exercise of our spirit we will be filled unto all the fullness of God to produce the church life.

Questions

1. Why can we say that the book of Ephesians shows us that the Body of Christ is related to our human spirit?

2. What is the problem with trying to understand the church with our mind?

3. Why is the building up of the church the result of turning to our spirit rather than lingering in our mind and emotions?

4. Why is our spirit in Ephesians 4 called the spirit of the mind?

5. What verses in Ephesians show us:
   a. The seeing in the spirit.
   b. The building up in the spirit.
   c. Being strengthened in the spirit.
   d. Being renewed in the spirit.
   e. Being filled in the spirit.

Quoted Portions
from (Lee/LSM) Publications

1. *Life-study of Ephesians,* p. 570.

2. *To Serve in the Human Spirit,* pp. 31, 32, 34, 36-40.

THE CONSUMMATE ISSUE
OF THE TWO SPIRITS

Scripture Reading

Rev. 1:12, 20; John 14:17-20; 16:13-15;
Rev. 22:17a; 1:2, 9; 19:7-10; 21:2, 9, 11, 18-21; 22:1-2, 14

Outline

I. The church
  A. The mingling of the divine life and the human life
  B. The lampstands—the embodiment of Christ and the reproduction of the Spirit
II. The New Jerusalem—the Spirit being one with the bride
  A. The universal marriage
  B. The mingling of the Trinity with His redeemed
    1. The Father's nature, the Son's redemption, and the Spirit's transformation
    2. The consummation of the divine dispensing
  C. To express God fully for eternity

Text

I. THE CHURCH

A. The Mingling of the Divine Life
and the Human Life

In the foregoing lessons [we pointed out that God's purpose is to obtain the church by dispensing Himself into man and making Himself one with man. In order to dispense Himself into man, God must be triune, the Father, the Son, and the Spirit. Furthermore, man must be in God's image and have a spirit to receive God and assimilate Him. One day, the Son of God, the embodiment of the Father, became a man. Passing through human living, crucifixion, and resurrection, He became the life-giving Spirit. As the

Spirit, He comes into us and mingles with our spirit. Through this process there is brought into being a hybrid life, an entity composed of the mingling of the divine life with the human life. This is the church.

God is no longer the unprocessed God, but the processed God. He has accomplished everything necessary to come into us as the life-giving Spirit. Now we must believe in Him and call on the name of the Lord Jesus. When we do this, the life-giving Spirit comes into our spirit, and the mingling of the divine life and human life takes place within us. This mingling produces the church.]

[Our experience testifies that the very Christ whom we enjoy each day is the life-giving Spirit. Do you not have the reality of the living One within you? This is the very Christ whom we are enjoying, experiencing, and partaking of in our spirit. This is the life-giving Spirit who is Christ Himself. Thus, God is embodied in Christ, and Christ is realized and experienced in us as the life-giving Spirit. This experience issues in the church. The more we experience Christ in this way, the more we long for the church.]

B. The Lampstands—the Embodiment of Christ and the Reproduction of the Spirit

In Revelation 1 the churches are seen as the seven golden lampstands. (See also Lessons 7 and 12 of the Triune God lesson book.)

[Christ is realized as the Spirit, and the Spirit is expressed as the churches. The shining Spirit is the reality of the shining Christ, and the shining churches are the reproduction and the expression of the shining Spirit to accomplish God's eternal purpose that the New Jerusalem as the shining city may be consummated. Christ, the Spirit, and the churches are all of the same divine nature.]

[The churches are the lampstands, and the lamps are the sevenfold intensified Spirit of God as the expression of Christ. This light is shining brighter and brighter, and the vision is becoming clearer every day.

The local churches as the golden lampstands shine with

such a Spirit in the dark age of today. In today's dark age, the church really needs the sevenfold intensified Spirit of God to shine forth the testimony of Jesus. The church is the embodiment of Christ and the reproduction of the Spirit. The Spirit is the reality of Christ (John 14:17-20; 16:13-15), and the church is the reproduction of the Spirit (Rev. 22:17a). The church with the Spirit is the embodiment of Christ, the testimony of Jesus (Rev. 1:2, 9; 19:10). Therefore, the more Spirit, the more church and the more testimony of Jesus.]

[The church is the embodiment of the Triune God dispensed into us and blended within us. It is the Triune God dispensed into humanity and blended in humanity as one single entity (Rev. 22:17a). There is no separation. This is the Spirit as the consummation of the Triune God, reaching His redeemed, and this is the consummation of the divine dispensing in this age.]

II. THE NEW JERUSALEM—
THE SPIRIT BEING ONE WITH THE BRIDE

[Eventually this consummation will come to the ultimate stage, the New Jerusalem. The New Jerusalem is a single entity which is considered the wife of the Lamb, the bride (Rev. 22:17).]

A. The Universal Marriage

[The consummation of the divine dispensing will be a universal marriage (Rev. 19:7-9; 21:2, 9). The Spirit as the consummation of the processed Triune God dispensed into His redeemed people will be there as the Bridegroom; and God's redeemed people as the consummation of the redeemed, regenerated, and transformed humanity will be there as the bride. We know this because Revelation 22:17 reads, "And the Spirit and the bride say, Come!" In this verse the Spirit and the bride together as a couple say "come." The husband is the Spirit, and the wife is the bride.]

B. The Mingling of the Trinity
with His Redeemed

1. The Father's Nature, the Son's Redemption, and the Spirit's Transformation

[The New Jerusalem is a composition of the divine Trinity with God's redeemed people. First of all it is composed of God the Father's nature, signified by the gold. The city and its street are made of pure gold (21:18, 21b), denoting God the Father in His nature. The twelve gates of the New Jerusalem, which are twelve pearls (21:21a), signify God the Son's overcoming death and His life-imparting resurrection. An oyster is a small animal which lives in the death waters. It has a life which overcomes the death waters, and by secreting a life element, it produces pearls. Christ's overcoming death plus His life-imparting resurrection secretes the "juice" of the divine life to form us into pearls. So in the pearl we can see the Son in His death and resurrection. The pearl signifies God's redeemed and regenerated people. According to John 3, regeneration is the entry into the kingdom. You cannot enter into the kingdom of God unless you are born of the Spirit (John 3:5). Regeneration is the entry, the gate, into the New Jerusalem.

The precious stones signify the transforming work of God the Spirit (Rev. 21:11, 18-20). After regeneration, the Spirit continues to transform the regenerated people of God to make every one of them a precious stone. By this you can see that the New Jerusalem is a composition of the Father as the substance, of the Son as the entry, and of the Spirit as the transformation. It is a building of the Trinity with redeemed, regenerated, and transformed humanity.]

2. The Consummation of the Divine Dispensing

[The entire New Jerusalem is saturated with God the Spirit as the river of living water which flows out of the throne of God the Father and of the Lamb, God the Son. In the river the tree of life grows (Rev. 22:1-2). The life water, God the Spirit, quenches thirst, and the life tree, God the Son, nourishes. The entire city, which is a composition of the

Trinity with His redeemed people, is watered, nourished, and saturated with the divine life, which is nothing less than the Triune God (Rev. 22:1-2, 14, 17), dispensing Himself to saturate His redeemed people. What a picture this is! This is a blending of the Triune God with His redeemed people. The nature of the Father is the substance. The redemption of the Son, including His death and resurrection, is the entry. And the Spirit's transformation is the work to make us divine and precious. Such a composition is the New Jerusalem. It is saturated by the eternal life, which is the Triune God Himself. This is the consummation of the divine dispensing.

I look to the Lord that through these messages you may see a vision of God's economy, God's goal, and what God is doing to reach His goal. What God is doing is dispensing Himself as the Father, the source, as the Son, the expression, and as the Spirit, the very entering in, into you and me. Day and night He is working on this one thing. He is working toward this one goal, that we all would be a lampstand in this age to express the Triune God, and eventually that we would be that bride in eternity, a composition of redeemed and regenerated humanity saturated with the Triune God as life.]

C. To Express God Fully for Eternity

[Such a composition of the Triune God with His redeemed people will express God fully for eternity (Rev. 21:11a). So at the end of the sixty-six books of the Bible, the Spirit is the ultimate consummation of the Triune God.

Now we can see why John says that the Son comes in the Father's name, and the Spirit comes in the Son's name. In his Gospel John prepares the way to show us that these three— the Father, the Son, and the Spirit—are not separate. These three actually are one. The source, the expression, and the entering in become the consummation. The Spirit is not separated from the Son nor from the Father. The Spirit is the consummation of the entire Triune God. The Spirit as the Bridegroom is the totality and consummation of the Triune God. He is qualified to be such a husband to marry the wife, who is the consummation of all the redeemed and regenerated people of God. This is a universal couple with divinity marrying humanity.

Here are two consummations. Divinity has gone through a process—through incarnation, through crucifixion, through resurrection, and through ascension—to become the Spirit, the totality, the consummation, of the Triune God to be the Bridegroom. Humanity also has gone through a process—through redemption, through regeneration, and through transformation—to become the consummation of God's chosen, redeemed, regenerated, and transformed people. The consummation of the Triune God and the consummation of God's chosen, redeemed, regenerated, and transformed people become one in a universal marriage. The processed man will match the processed God forever for His full expression and satisfaction.]

SUMMARY

The processed Triune God as the life-giving Spirit dispenses Himself into man and mingles with man to produce the church. Because the Spirit is the reality of Christ, the more we are mingled with the Spirit, the more we become the embodiment of Christ. We also become the lampstands shining with the sevenfold intensified Spirit in a dark age as the testimony of Jesus. The mingling eventually consummates in the New Jerusalem, where the Spirit as the Bridegroom and the church as the bride are joined in a universal marriage. The New Jerusalem as the consummate issue of the Triune God dispensed into man will express the Triune God for eternity.

Questions

1. What does "consummate issue" mean?

2. How does the Triune God mingle Himself with man to produce the church?

3. How do the golden lampstands in Revelation 1 show us that the churches are the embodiment of Christ and the reproduction of the Spirit?

4. Since the New Jerusalem is not a physical city, what does it symbolize?

5. What do the gold, pearl, and precious stones signify in the New Jerusalem?

6. Regarding the universal marriage in Revelation:
   a. Who is the Bridegroom?
   b. Who is the bride?
   c. What is the process that the Bridegroom has gone through?
   d. What is the process that the bride has gone through?

Quoted Portions
from (Lee/LSM) Publications

1. *Life-study of Ephesians,* p. 573.

2. *Life-study of Revelation,* pp. 85-86, 93, 99.

3. *The Divine Dispensing of the Divine Trinity,* pp. 41-44.

BOOKS IN THIS SERIES
Living Stream Ministry

Lesson Book, Level 1:
    God's Full Salvation   0-87083-521-1

Lesson Book, Level 2:
    The Triune God and
        the Person and Work of Christ   0-87083-522-X

Lesson Book, Level 3:
    The Two Spirits—
    The Divine Spirit and the Human Spirit
                                             0-87083-523-8

Lesson Book, Level 4:
    Knowing and Experiencing Life   0-87083-524-6

Lesson Book, Level 5:
    The Church—
    The Vision and Building Up of the Church
                                             0-87083-525-4

Lesson Book, Level 6:
    The Bible—The Word of God   0-87083-594-7

Available at
Christian bookstores, or contact Living Stream Ministry
2431 W. La Palma Ave. • Anaheim, CA 92801
1-800-549-5164 • www.livingstream.com